RESILIENT AMERICANS

WE MAY NOT HAVE IT ALL TOGETHER,
BUT TOGETHER WE HAVE IT ALL

Diane Burden Cox

Positively Powered Publications

Author: Diane Burden Cox

Book Cover Design: Melody Christian, Finicky Designs

Editor: Amy Collette

Positively Powered Publications
Denver, CO

positivelypoweredauthors.com

Ordering Information: Quantity sales. Special discounts are available on quantity purchases by corporations, associations, and others. For details, contact us at positivelypoweredauthors.com.

Resilient Americans/ Diane Burden Cox. —1st ed.

ISBN 978-0-9961692-8-8

Contents

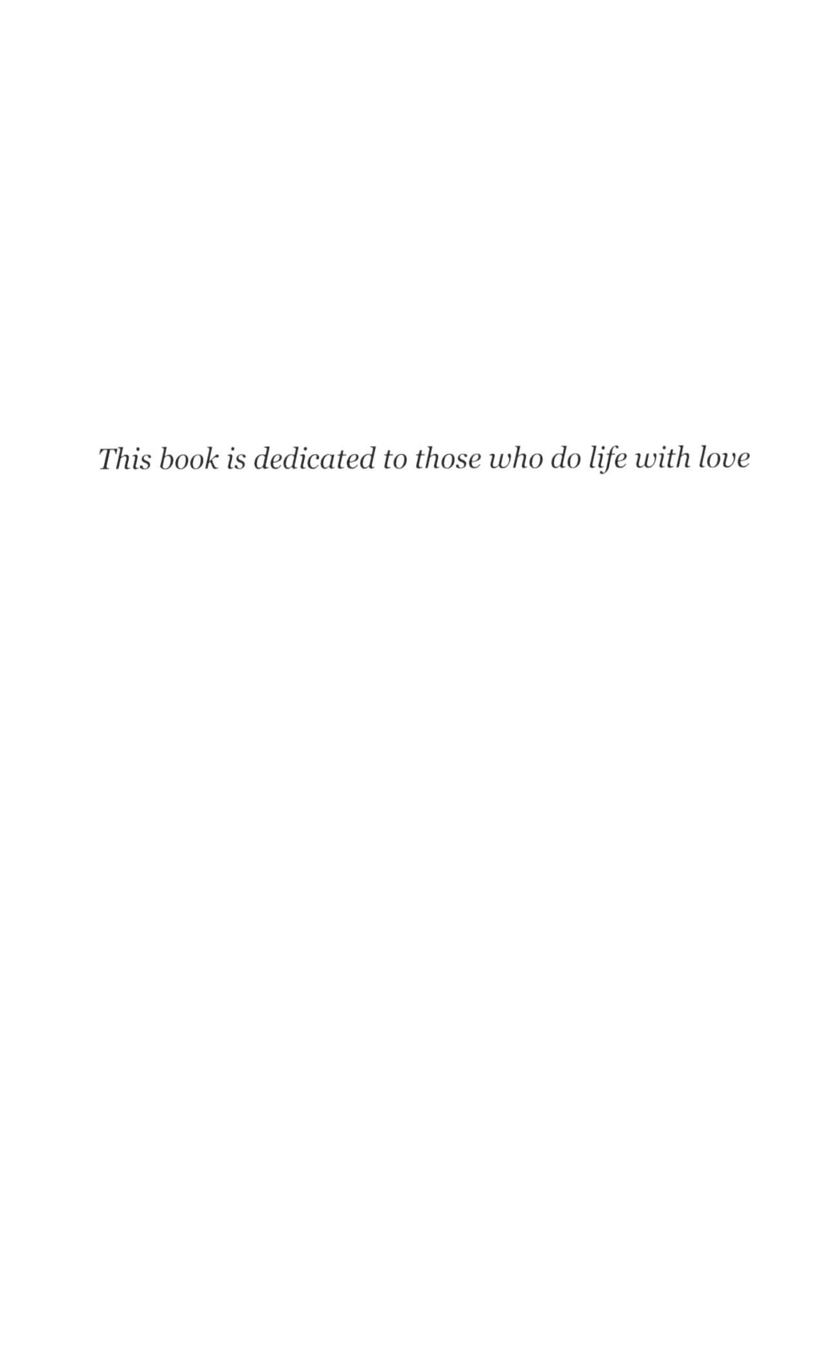

This book is dedicated to those who do life with love

Hey There

I would have titled this *Preface*, but then a lot of you would have skipped it.

Bear with me. This may not be the book you thought you'd find inside *Resilient Americans*. We have certain expectations when the topics of resilience, disasters and Americans are being discussed. We think we'll learn interesting details about a major catastrophe, see how individuals or groups of citizens were strong in the face of overwhelming challenges and maybe hear some lessons from survivors and their rescuers.

This isn't that.

I wrote this book because I've learned a lot from running a disaster consulting firm. I want people to see the direct connection between how we all choose to live our daily lives and the strength of our nation. Living in this time when there are more and increasingly costly natural and man-made disasters can help us focus on what's most important and what we can each do to make our country resilient.

The work my husband, Graeme, and I do in the federal and state systems of disaster recovery is not the same as the adrenaline-pumping, attention-getting work you see on TV and in the movies. That's the disaster response phase. Response gets politicians and journalists excited and is part and parcel of popular culture.

The disaster recovery phase is all documentation, damage assessments and federal funding. It's boring, detailed work with long hours and bureaucratic muddle in places the country has mostly forgotten by the time the recovery labor force is showing up. But, working on recovery is also a great way to see America with the veneer pulled back. Who we are and how we've built our country is what you see when you're part of the team trying to put things back together after pieces of it have been shaken, blown down, washed away or burned.

But as much as I've learned from years in the world of disaster recovery, I've learned even more from decades of ordinary living. Think of this book as the beginning of a happy dinnertime with friends and family. It has more anecdotes and stories than disaster fundamentals. It didn't start out that way, but as I wrote, it became evident that my beliefs about resilience began a long time before I became part of the disaster industry. The best thing any of us can bring to our national dinner table conversation about being strong and overcoming crises is who we are. There is no resilient America without resilient Americans.

Dead Ducks and a Whack in the Head

I was pacing with a crying baby in our home in Sacramento, looking out the living room window when I saw my neighbor, Glenn, pull up to his house across the street. I watched him get out of his car, walk to the back, open the trunk, and pull out a shotgun with his left hand and a string of dead ducks with his right. I was shocked, not so much at the sight of the gun, although I felt a second of dread, or even by the beautiful animals hanging limp and lifeless, but because Glenn was the regional director of the Audubon Society, an organization I thought existed for the *protection* of birds. It appeared to me that our friend was some sort of crazy hypocrite.

As it turns out, I was right and wrong; Audubon was founded to protect bird populations, only in different ways than I had assumed. Glenn was not a fraud by killing the birds he worked to protect. Invited for a duck dinner at their house, the apparent contradiction began to clear as we learned about scientifically based wildlife conservation, the restoration of natural ecosystems and how focusing on birds and their habitats benefit people and the world's biodiversity. We also learned that some of the most generous donations to this nonprofit effort came from duck hunters who, aware of diminishing habitat and bird populations, were motivated to protect and invest in wetland conservation.

My initial view of my neighbor's seemingly inconsistent behavior illustrates an important point: most topics are best understood using more than a two-dimensional frame of reference. How something looks on paper might be called "factual," but is often flat, shallow and oversimplified. Two dimensions cannot accommodate living, breathing human life. We need to make space in our thinking for more dimensions if we hope to understand both the world around us and the people in it. We need to continue to learn and dialogue about what we *think* we know until we come to those larger understandings that are only available to us together.

When my son Andrew was just over 2 and Ryan was only a few months old, we were at a park with other moms and little ones. I was attending to Ryan when I looked up just in time to see Andrew get up from the sandbox and run delightedly toward a friend he had spotted in a swing. I jumped up, handing Ryan off to another mom as Andrew ran, arms spread wide, toward his friend who was swinging away from him. Little Andrew didn't understand the pendulum concept and wasn't prepared to have the swing with his friend come rushing back toward him. The metal safety bar of the swing hit Andrew's head and knocked him to the ground. As I scooped him up, his hair was already covered with blood. Aching with empathy, I comforted him and tried to assess how badly he was injured. After a trip to the emergency room and help with cleaning the wound, we were assured he was fine and that the dramatic amount of blood had more to do with the number of blood vessels in the human head than the severity of the injury.

I've thought of that swing in the years since because it illustrates what it's like to approach complex issues with dualistic thinking. Binary reasoning is a potentially deadly pendulum. Trying to address complex issues with only two choices is likely to get you a whack in the head.

That's not to say that there's no value in considering, for instance, what is hateful versus what is loving. There can be more clarity when difficulties are simplified to their essence, and sometimes there are only two sides to the proverbial coin. But, Graeme and I often talk about pulling the bolt out of the fixed point that's holding us to the pendulum effect in our heated discussions when we catch ourselves getting stuck. Any mutually beneficial course of action can remain invisible if our thinking only moves in an arc, caught between two extremes. Solutions are usually found higher up.

We don't need to be constrained by only two choices, yours or mine, red or blue, left or right. These are often insufficient for addressing the difficulties present in our world today. There are spheres of perspectives surrounding most issues. There are many angles from which the same challenge can be seen. One of the beautiful things about the US is that we are a people with enough unique perspectives to view most issues from all sides. We are a very big "us." To be resilient, we need to cultivate a willingness to see more than two options and work to discover the beautifully complex, multi-dimensional landscape of possibilities we have when we put our heads together.

Getting Out of the Trenches

One of our family's favorite movies is *Joyeux Noel*. It's based on the history of what happened between some of the soldiers in the foxholes of France one Christmas during World War I. In the movie, soldiers from opposing armies, weary of fighting, far from loved ones and longing for the basic comforts of home, unexpectedly create an impromptu truce and develop human connections with their enemies. On what had been the field of battle, they gathered together and played soccer. These soldiers wanted the war to end, and after that Christmas Day of being together they desired to continue the truce; their leaders and governments did not. The men, having become aware of how much they had in common with each other, preferred the position of friendship to the posture of war.

I believe America has a hopeful future and we will find it together, in the sum of our parts, through what we all have in common and those unique things we each have to contribute. I believe we all view the world through the windows of our interior space. We are each of us looking out from our unique trenches constructed of our DNA, developmental experiences, culture and particular spirit. In these pages, I share pieces of my story, some from childhood, some from work in disaster recovery management, with the intention of encouraging us to recognize the importance of one another's stories as we move forward together.

In the movie about that Christmas in World War I, even though many of them did not speak the same languages, the men sang carols, shared pictures and pantomimed stories of their wives and families. They drank together and ate food sent from loved ones back home, talked about cafés, restaurants and hotels they had enjoyed in the others' countries, and played games. I believe the power of our dynamic, democratic republic is found in the heart of friendship, friendly dialogue and play—those simple, human places where we relax, share something of ourselves and enjoy one another's company.

I'm not claiming to be an expert on any of the themes here: friendship, developmental psychology, community resilience, disasters, infrastructure recovery, diversity, the arts, education, religion, media or government. I *am* claiming, with a smile, to be relatively expert on my own life and the things I've experienced. I think all of our life stories, our collective experiences and the wisdom we gain as we mature, practice our skills and crafts, move through careers, raise families and generally engage with the world around us, are at least as important as the opinions of experts.

Within the people of America are the answers to America's problems. Programs, organizations, systems and resources obviously have their place, but "we the people" are ultimately our greatest asset. We keep missing that.

A first step toward mutual understanding often requires taking a step back, the way a photographer steps back to include more of the surroundings. What if each of us stepped back and allowed a wider lens when we're sharing our opinions and stating our positions on particular issues? We need to understand one another's convictions in the context of our stories so that we gain the additional wisdom not available to us in our solitary truths.

I have certainly felt frustration and even anger with people who think differently than I do. I have also learned that my negative and harmful emotions decrease when I take the time to listen to another person who is willing to share authentically from their story. When I reciprocate with my own tales and they hear mine, we often gain a desire to find solutions that are mutually beneficial as we begin to feel a sense of connection.

We're in need of détente in America, an era of relaxed and good-natured discourse. We need hope-filled discussions in classrooms and boardrooms that end in collaboration instead of competition, for teamwork that crosses the aisle, and for respectful gatherings at round tables. But even more, we the people are in need of casual conversations around campfires, laughter at shared meals, and time together on our figurative playgrounds where we meet not to judge whether the other is right or wrong, but to share our stories, get to know one another, and find out how our unique experiences have shaped our opinions, beliefs, and the courage of our convictions. If we choose to move in the direction of caring about one another's experiences and stories, we will find we're moving in the direction of the solutions we need to address the daunting problems facing our nation and the world.

Whackadoodles

Definition of a whackadoodle: An eccentric or fanatical person.

There was a Saturday Night Live skit years ago where Gilda Radner played a character, Miss Litella, on a newscast. She was a classic whackadoodle. She would rant on about an issue only to discover she was completely misinformed about the crucial point. When corrected, she would turn to the camera and simply say, "I'm sorry, never mind." Like so many one-liners from SNL skits, this phrase became part of the culture.

Sometimes we can be almost maniacally convinced our particular perspective is the one and only right way. Each of us has certainly had moments of thinking that the position where I stand, looking out from my head and assessing the reality of the world around me, is the singular and precise position of clear thinking and all pertinent facts. That's why I like this word whackadoodle. I use it to describe folks who appear overly confident and loudly vocal about their opinions. I am a whackadoodle at times myself.

Whackadoodles feel a compelling need to get people to agree with them. They put the pressure on during conversations, often using demeaning and insulting language or an angry tone of voice in hopes of conforming others to their will and making them think like they do. Some stay quietly aloof, assured of the accuracy of their stance, unwilling to risk the peace of their private certitude. Other whackadoodles use humor at other people's expense to try to get the upper hand.

While sarcastic humor can be witty and requires a fair amount of intelligence, it rarely belongs where we need to work together at solving the world's problems. Derived from the Greek, the word sarcasm literally means "to tear flesh." Hope for creating unity when we're cutting one another apart isn't likely. We may be laughing, but I doubt if derisive or scornful laughter actually lifts our spirits or moves us in the direction where hope lies. I'm fairly confident it doesn't create the healthy connections that come when people are able to really laugh together in enjoyment or delight. As the word sounds to the ear, sarcasm is more likely to create a chasm between us than build the bridges we need to be resilient.

When I was a young teen, I remember my parents coming home from listening to a seminary professor. They told us about the crazy tension in the room when a man jumped up in the middle of the lecture, challenging the speaker by exclaiming, "That's not what you believe!"

They said the professor had reasserted with good humor that he actually did believe what he was saying. But, the man wouldn't be put off. Holding up a book written by the professor some years before and waving it to emphasize his words, he said accusingly, "Well that's not what you said in here!"

All heads swiveled back to the front to see how this confrontation was going to go. Cocking his head to one side, the professor smiled, "Well then, I guess I changed my mind." Somewhat mollified, the man sat down.

My parents enjoyed his self-deprecating sense of humor. Of course, the story only works as an example of how not to be a whackadoodle as long as the professor was acknowledging that his thinking had changed or was evolving since writing the book. If instead, he was speaking out of both sides of his mouth or being deceitful in some way, then he, not the guy interrupting, would be the whackadoodle in that exchange.

Still, I like the point this story makes. We could stand to take ourselves less seriously. We aren't any of us getting it all right all of the time. Those who are able to laugh at themselves instead of demeaning others are assets during crisis and are resilient community members. While convinced of their own point of view, they are aware that even their own understanding or perspective is a work in progress. They learn, grow, change and become wiser. They're able to listen and converse with people of different opinions, working together to find the places of connection, mutual compromise and compassionate outcomes. Simply put, they don't behave like whackadoodles.

If we tell each other our stories, explaining a bit of how we came to think as we do, knowing we don't know it all, and we're willing to humbly quote Miss Litella on occasion, we'll have fewer whackadoodle moments gumming up our visionary discussions and problem-solving dialogues.

You may think I'm whacky, but I really, really think I'm right about that.

Northridge Earthquake

The ringing telephone in the kitchen forced me out of bed and stumbling into the chill of a dark Northern California winter morning. I picked up the receiver on the phone above the highchair and heard my sister Linda say, "We just had a really big earthquake in LA. I think it's going to be bad this time."

In the next hours, we heard from different family members and friends, calling to let us know, thankfully, they were safe and that most of their homes and businesses had experienced relatively minor damage.

On Martin Luther King, Jr's Holiday, January 17, 1994, a "moderate" 6.7 earthquake hit Los Angeles County and caused over $40 billion in damages. My husband, Graeme, and I had a small engineering and construction company in Sacramento at the time and were living 400 miles north of the epicenter with our three young sons in a solid little bungalow on 38th Street. After all the phone calls assuring us that those we knew and loved were doing well, we were able to return to our daily rhythms while we watched the news of lives lost, destroyed freeways, schools, hospitals and homes, and the ongoing response efforts in Southern California.

A couple of months later, we heard through a neighbor that the California Governor's Office of Emergency Services (OES) was looking for engineers to work for six months on recovery efforts in Los Angeles out of an office close to where our parents and other family lived. Graeme faxed an application and was hired. We decided to rent out our house for a year and move. While it would only be temporary work on the earthquake, Graeme was grateful to be of help to the region we grew up in and we were delighted that our kids would have some time living near their grandparents.

Weeks after the initial response phase of the disaster, Graeme showed up for his first day of work at one of the three offices established by the Federal Emergency Management Agency (FEMA) and OES for the Northridge Earthquake recovery. He was surprised to find a significant amount of emergency chaos still existed on the crowded floor, where hundreds of staff were coordinating recovery projects.

As the only orientation to what appeared to be anything but a smoothly functioning recovery, Graeme was handed an almost illegible copy of the Federal Register and told to read it. Looking for an empty desk or place to sit, Graeme ended up in a stairwell puzzling over the record, searching for what it had to do with the Northridge Earthquake. He felt a sense of dismay, wondering if he'd made a mistake by agreeing to contribute to something this disorganized and inefficient. How in the world was he going to help anyone? For an engineer wired for straightforward equations and efficiency, the Joint Field

Office with all its disarray, layers of bureaucracy and government regulations was a challenging place.

Finally, after reading through several pages of what seemed completely unrelated changes, he found a reference having to do with a congressional amendment to the Robert T. Stafford Disaster and Relief and Emergency Assistance Act. He would eventually discover that the Stafford Act is the legal backbone to FEMA's Public Assistance responsibilities. But in that moment, the words on the page had little meaning and no practical application.

Graeme had shown up to work, carrying a sense of hope that he'd be making a real difference like many of us want to do, not just during disasters, but also with our lives in general. Yet, as he came out of the stairwell to find out what his next task would be, his idealism was fading. Eventually that day, he was given some damage survey reports to go over, scrounged for a pen so he could make notes and returned to the stairwell. He was disappointed. The professional world of disaster recovery in America was a lot different than he'd expected, but he decided he was going to stay and try to make a positive impact.

Moving Beyond
Disaster to Us

THEMES: • We can listen & learn from where others are coming from (Front lines)
• Assumptions about "normal" Expectations
• Nobody's an expert in how this impacts every part of everyday life.

Imagine how different tomorrow would be if you woke up to discover your home, local stores, gas stations, children's schools, and your place of business had no water or sewer service and it would take weeks before it was restored.

Many of us go about our daily lives assuming there are strength and resilience in the world that's below our feet, in our walls and moving around us. We've come to expect everything foundational to our lifestyles to function well simply because we make monthly payments for our utilities. Yet, after a major disaster like the Northridge Earthquake, water and sewer systems are only two aspects of our assumed daily resilience that disappear in moments. The same is true for every other type of disaster and every other system we rely on for our existence and wellbeing.

Graeme's inauspicious beginnings in 1994 in the stairwell were followed by years working as an OES Public Assistance Program Manager for Southern California on a variety of disasters—earthquakes, fires, storms, mudslides—along with a backlog of recovery issues that occurred prior to the Northridge Earthquake. He believed his work mattered and he was making a difference. He enjoyed what he did and the people he worked with and over the years many colleagues became our friends.

In October 2003, as many devastating fires burned through Southern California, Sacramento decided to downsize the OES office in L.A. Graeme and other staff lost their jobs. The fires seemed to emphasize our loss and gave us extra empathy for those suffering in the disasters. Firefighters were finding it impossible to stop or even slow the destruction, and the air throughout the region was filled with eye-stinging smoke, obscuring the landscape with grey ash. We were hearing personal stories of tragedy from friends who had lost their homes, neighborhoods and businesses.

Graeme and I felt disheartened because he and his colleagues at OES were no longer in a position to help with recovery efforts. When the state left the JFO that October, the team that dispersed took with them extensive institutional wisdom acquired through hard experience about how the system worked best to accomplish what it was originally designed to do—restore function to public infrastructure. The loss of recovery personnel in Southern California left a hole we thought needed to be filled.

As a result, Graeme and I decided to start our own business so that he could keep assisting local entities impacted by the fires and others, like LA Unified School District, which still had ongoing recovery efforts from the Northridge Earthquake. Soon we also began working on a variety of federally declared disasters around the nation and have been in the disaster field ever since. We make a good team, Graeme using his engineering, construction, and FEMA Public Assistance background, and me, using what I know of sociology, psychology and education to understand the impacts of disaster.

Being disaster consultants can sound a lot more interesting than it is. Our consulting firm is one of the many cogwheels in the huge and complicated mechanism of the business of disaster in America. Over the years our company has worked in different parts of the country on Hurricanes like Katrina in Louisiana, Ike and Harvey in Texas, and Irene and Sandy in New York. We've helped with major floods and ice storms in Midwestern and Southern states, and on recovery efforts in the West from earthquakes, fires and mudslides.

We try to keep our answers short and succinct when people ask us what, specifically, our company does. Simply put, the bulk of our work has been as emergency management technical support during the recovery phase of federal disasters. We become part of the bureaucracy that is in place in the United States to transfer federal funds to the state and local disaster recovery efforts. We help with the assessment of infrastructure damage and the application of laws, regulations and policies.

In everyday language, the FEMA Public Assistance work we do is part building inspector, part insurance adjuster, and part lawyer.

Our work has given us experience looking at what factors and attributes contribute to the resilience of buildings, utilities, hospitals, schools, dams, levees and other infrastructure. We've also had opportunities to learn from and contribute to discussions with academics, responders, hospital administrators, food bank managers, engineers, business owners, scientists, political leaders, and many others involved in rebuilding and improving disaster resilience.

The complexity of our infrastructure continues to grow as we advance technologically without a comparable increase in the resilience of the systems we require to maintain our current quality of life. As a result of working on every type of disaster and from countless conversations, one of the things we've learned is that there is broad professional consensus across all industries and disciplines: the nation must invest in strengthening the public infrastructure we all totally rely on and yet take for granted.

Even so, as much as our work has taught us the importance of America's public infrastructure, the two of us have come to recognize the even greater value of the *people* who make up our communities, and who build, operate and use the infrastructure that forms the bedrock of our lives. We need to move beyond simply trying to fix our stuff. We need to acknowledge the primary importance that *who we are* underlies and shapes our nation's built infrastructure.

Graeme and I are persuaded that to become a country that is truly resilient, we the people must have a collective change of heart. The best way to do that is to build an understanding of who we are. We need to know something about where we're each coming from before we will be able to collaborate and work together to create a positive vision for where we want to go and how we'll get there. The easiest way to begin is by sharing our various stories that have shaped us and the way we think.

I'll go first...

We're Each Unique

Holding on tight to the chains, my mom pushed me, telling me to lean in before stretching out flat and thrusting my feet upward. I was learning to pump so I could gain height on our swing set. When I was 3 years old, our backyard in San Diego was on the upper edge of a small hill. My view from my swinging perch that morning in 1961 felt lofty and expansive, filled with sky and clouds. As I leaned back and flung my feet up toward the sky, I asked, "Mommy, who made the clouds?"

"God made the clouds, sweetheart."

My family tells stories when we get together. The memories we recall usually remind us of good times, help us laugh at ourselves or portray how we learned something. Mom tells this cloud story to explain how she and Dad decided to find a church to go to after years of absence. In that quiet moment alone with me in the backyard, Mom became aware, after her reflexive answer, of how uncertain she felt about the difficult questions ahead as she raised her children. Her mother had died when she was only 11 years old, and lacking a maternal presence she could turn to, Mom decided she needed something more to draw on than her current life experience and abilities to be a good mother. We can really only contribute to the world what we receive or learn ourselves.

While I don't recall our conversation about clouds, I have a convincing gut level memory of the joy of flight on that little swing set and the sense that mother love, God, and flying free in the vastness of the sky belonged together.

Some people might think the last place to find wisdom is in religion. Thankfully, my parents were more interested in relationship than the rules they associated with their childhood experiences in church. By this time, my dad was already working in aerospace at General Dynamics, so I imagine he could have offered a more scientific explanation about the origin of clouds. I'm glad that's not how that moment in our family's history was resolved. I don't think my 3-year-old self was asking about cloud physics.

Our stories about how we developed our understanding of concepts like family, religion, education, health, politics and many other topics are relevant in how we each see our world. Our personal development stories, our perceptions and conclusions from childhood underlie our usually unspoken life philosophies. Our current standpoint and overarching worldview are often the result of our unique upbringing, education and life experiences.

Other family stories are the tabs on the file folders of my developing identity.

One day as my mom was hanging the laundry outside the kitchen window, I was inside pointing to a bowl of frosting she had just made for a cake still in the oven. The mixing bowl was out of her line of sight and she imagined I was pointing at the box of graham crackers she left on the table. She thought another wouldn't hurt, so she smiled and nodded, "Yes, go ahead."

When she came back into the kitchen, she found most of the frosting gone and me holding a large spoon, looking green around the gills. I remember hanging over the toilet bowl, miserable and absolutely convinced that too much frosting was a bad, bad thing. Who would have thought? It had been one of my favorites. It didn't put me off all dessert or even frosting. But to this day I am a moderate consumer.

When we moved from San Diego to Altadena when I was 4, I left my rough-and-tumble neighbors, Billy and Jed, behind, and was introduced to my new neighbor, Kathy. On the first day we played together, Mom threw a large sheet over the dining room table to create a playhouse for the two of us, and went back into the kitchen. She was happy to hear me take the lead as hostess, establishing the ground rules for playing house, "Okay, you can be the mommy..."

And then to my mother's surprise, I roared, "And I'll be the tiger that comes and tears your house down!"

Evidently there was an adjustment period as Kathy learned to be a little more adventurous and I calibrated my enthusiasm to a more sedate imaginary world where mommies and daddies cooked food, went on trips, and took care of stuffed animal children.

Children learn and form ideas about the nature of the world and their place in it from a myriad of experiences, observations and interactions. Play is an important tool in sorting them out. Children's self-awareness and their perspective on the world and people usually grow progressively.

Mom recalls hearing me march up and down the length of the living room not long after the tiger incident, my arms swinging stiffly at my sides as I planted each step with loud military precision. She came in to let me know I needed to tone things down. She didn't want me to wake up my little sister.

Mom asked, referring to the foil-wrapped Christmas candy we had bought together that morning, "Are you pretending to be a chocolate soldier?"

I answered, "No, I this color," and raised my arm, pinching my pink baby skin between my index finger and thumb to show her.

My mom says she knew I was referencing the variety of skin colors. It tickled her to think that I saw the world of people around me as candy. I still hold a deep, blurry childhood awareness of people as favorite flavors. Our individual understandings about the world are as varied and different as there are people in it.

Adults Help Shape Our Views

We moved into my mother's childhood home in Altadena, California in 1963 when I was 5. I have many clear memories of my life there that are twined together with the stories I heard about earlier happenings in that little white cottage when my mom was a girl. Dad grew up about a mile away and through the memories that he, my mom and my grandparents shared, the neighborhoods, orange groves and horse stables of Altadena and Pasadena during the Depression, World War II, and early post-war years came alive. The entertaining stories my parents and grandparents told about their childhoods contributed to my growing sense of my place in the world at large.

I remember my required nap times being unwelcome by that age. Happily, I soon discovered that my parents' bed, where I was put down to sleep in the middle of the day, was close enough to my father's highboy dresser that with a few acrobatics, I could raid his top drawer to pilfer a candy out of his Pez dispenser. I took only one piece each day. It was easy to restrain myself to one since after the frosting incident there was no way I wanted to repeat a horrible sugar overdose. I worked to make the piece of candy last by trying not to chew. It made nap time go quicker and seem sweeter.

However, it wasn't long before I realized that hiding small thievery could add up to bigger trouble. I have a visceral memory of the prickles of dismay I felt the day I took a candy and realized I had emptied Popeye of all his treats. I felt panicked when I couldn't figure out how to get that last little candy brick back into the dispenser. The flat plastic interior accused me and my overly sensitive conscience. I sat down and ate the evidence in quiet misery, certain in the knowledge there would be a spanking when my crime was discovered. Somehow, I was never found out, but because of that Pez dispenser in Dad's top drawer, I gained a built-in conviction that it was wrong to take the smallest thing that wasn't mine.

I recall being punished another time for saying something offensive enough that Mom marched me into the bathroom, grabbed a bar of soap, and told me to stick out my tongue. The nature of parenthood is that it's an art form mostly figured out by trial and error. My mom, sisters and I laugh about or bemoan the different "motherhood fails" we've committed with the best of intentions. This was one of Mom's. As I obediently stuck out my tongue, I knew with a child's intuition that I was looking up into the face of an adult who didn't have the foggiest idea what she was doing. Slowed down by her confusion, Mom tentatively swiped the soap over my tongue. I stood there, tongue hanging out, wondering what came next.

Mom paused, soap in hand, looking at me, and said, "Um... close your mouth and... hmm... and swallow."

I did as I was told, puzzled by this transaction, grimaced and gagged. Mom told me to spit in the sink as she quickly put toothpaste on my brush. I brushed with the minty goodness and she handed me a cup of water to rinse and spit.

Later that day, Mom was washing my hair in the kitchen sink, the method she used to keep the sting of shampoo out of sensitive eyes. She put a folded bath towel on the tiles and had me lie down on my back in the old kitchen where she had been a child, doing the same with her mother.

As she cradled my head, letting the warm water pour over my scalp, she told me she loved me. She laughed with me about how she hadn't known what she was doing earlier when she tried teaching me a lesson with the soap. I also remember her telling me that day about the friendship and love of Jesus who made even our worst mistakes come out right. To my growing understanding was added the confidence that God was a smiling parent, a presence like warm water that washes and soothes.

The peaceful, secure and resilient aspects of our identity are laid down like rows of brick in a house's wall, line upon line. So are the vulnerable and tender aspects. We become who we are in part because of the things we learn and take in, the stories we absorb from the world around us. In our early years of life, the things we experience in our family, at childcare or school, what we hear and see from an increasing deluge of media sources and technologies, and the reflection of ourselves we encounter as others interact with us, incrementally and imperceptibly contribute to our identity, shaping our definitions of concepts we later use to frame the world as we see it as adults. Our personal dictionaries and lexicons of meaning consciously and unconsciously reference the first usages and connotations crafted when our brains were most malleable.

Many in my generation remember our parents' sorrow and distress in 1963, following President John F. Kennedy's assassination. I was 5 and had started kindergarten two months before. My recollection of the impact of this national tragedy is woven together with the disappointment of missing the few television shows I was allowed to watch, as the news preempted regularly scheduled programming. My sadness in those days following this national disaster mostly came from the loss of the enjoyable aspects of my new school routine. Since all my needs continued to be met and the adults in my life, though visibly saddened and attuned to the national mourning, were resilient and maintained their functionality, I really didn't suffer any consequences.

On the other hand, when adults are disturbed by events, whether personal or communal, and are unable to remain functional, attentive and caring, children feel the turmoil and experience their own sense of loss and disturbance. The world as the child knows it reshapes and changes meaning around the event and the adults' incapacity. Their sense of safety, order and security can be negatively and even severely impacted.

Children's energy is best spent on unconcerned, healthy growth of mind and body, mostly unaware of grownup worries and concerns. Childhood needs play space for developing gradually toward resilient independence and adulthood. Trouble in whatever form can interfere with healthy development. But harsh circumstances don't necessarily prevent growth and resilience. For many reasons, we come into the world disproportionately able to handle difficulties. Also, teachers, grandparents, daycare workers and different adults who populate a child's life can help children retain a state of wellbeing.

The ways the adults respond to children's needs, from skinned knees to larger crises, assist in building strength and fortitude in children as they mature. Healthy and functioning family, a thriving and secure school and neighborhood life can contribute to resilience by helping children handle both positive and challenging experiences well. Our resilience as a country begins with the positive care and opportunities we give all our children.

School and Other Ways We Learn

I looked at the beautiful open box of eight large, new crayons Dr. Phyllis Roberts was holding out across her desk and named the colors, "Black, brown, red, orange, yellow, green, blue, and purple."

"Good, Diane, you're so smart! You're going to do well in school here."

Wow. It felt great to be smart. Until that day, I hadn't known I was. But if the principal, sitting behind her big desk in the first business office I had ever been in, said I was smart, it must be true. I had been nervous about going to meet Dr. Roberts to see if I was ready to start kindergarten, but after some small talk, counting to ten and passing this last test with flying colors, I was excited. School was going to be fun!

Because of the welcome I received that day, the simplicity of tests that were conversational and relational, and my parents' enthusiasm, I was given a basic, positive framework for understanding what school was. It served me well throughout my time in academics. Before I ever understood what the task of learning would be, I was told

I was in the right place, had what it took, and was going to succeed.

Pasadena Christian, the small, private school I would attend from kindergarten through eighth grade, became a happy extension of family and my overall sense of belonging. With a class size of about 20 and only 2 classes per grade, I spent elementary school and junior high with solid friendships in a secure and very disciplined academic environment. In those first years as a student, because of the consistency in my home, school, church, neighborhood, and also what I picked up from radio and television, I viewed the world I lived in as coherent and filled with mostly kind, considerate and reasonable human beings.

Our interactions shape our understanding and definitions in ways that are fundamental, foundational and often unconscious. Though we live in the same country, we each have unique experiences that shape our perceptions and lay the groundwork for our beliefs and assumptions about how the world works. As we go through life, we continue to interpret events, building on our earlier understandings.

"I heard a band of pirates buried secret treasure in the sandbox! Let's go!"

One of the first friends I made in kindergarten was Julie. She had an exceptional imagination, and like me, came from a family happy to help give playtime a boost with costumes and props. I have a favorite memory from recess of using magnets we brought to school to pull "black gold" from the sand. When we moved our magnets through the beige silica, iron filings would separate from the ordinary looking earth and we'd gather and put the fine, feathery, black particles into a small box. When recess was over, we would rebury our growing stash next to the big eucalyptus tree that shaded that part of the playground to be unearthed the next day in a new story of make-believe. Julie, our friends, and I were alternately explorers, pirates, cowhands or Indians in search of or protecting our treasure trove.

Our imaginary stories were persuasive and blended seamlessly with real life. Julie's grandparents, Roy Rogers and Dale Evans, were movie and television stars and looked and acted much like they appeared on their TV show. They lived on a ranch not far from Julie's home, just like my grandparents lived near me not far from the large farms where Granddad supervised harvests for Pasadena's frozen food plant. Her grandparents were cowboys; my grandparents were farmers. Both of our grandfathers wore cowboy hats to work to keep the sun off and cowboy boots that protected their feet. To my mind, these were practical work uniforms, not costumes.

When I went to Disneyland for the first time, the entire park seemed a magical playground for children about the real world. There were streetcars, theaters, stores and restaurants with fun rides woven throughout. When I was a girl, Indian Village was next to Frontierland and was a favorite attraction. The area had Native American homes and different American Indian tribes took turns demonstrating ceremonial dances in authentic dress. The Native American staff would explain traditions and symbols, and invite children to join them in dancing. I thought I was learning from friends of Julie's grandparents. After all, I had seen on TV how Roy Rogers and Dale Evans were always friends with the Indians. I came home from Disneyland with a new repertoire of dance moves gained from

Indian friends and a few new words I learned from Chief White Horse to add to our imaginary play. The world around me was caring, full and diverse, with intriguing new experiences and people. I belonged. I was surrounded by many nurturing adults who continued to intentionally and unintentionally shape my growing understanding of love and community.

Children absorb the mood of those around them and take in information they happen to encounter, creating a picture or understanding of the world. They develop a comprehension of the way things work using the puzzle pieces of their daily experiences.

My sixth birthday was an especially big deal because I finally needed two hands to communicate my maturity. There is a small, black-and-white photograph of seven little white girls on the front porch of my mother's childhood home, with several of us wearing kimonos and the others in more traditional 1960s "dress up" costumes.

I remember feeling especially pretty that day. There was something about wearing that flowered kimono that felt important and grown up like the women I admired in pictures. Julie had had her birthday before mine and celebrated with an eclectic Asian theme that included kimonos, tea, eating with chopsticks, Chinese jump rope, boxes of candy wrapped in sugared rice paper, and an assortment of brightly colored parasols and fabrics as decorations. Evidently, we were still enjoying imaginary stories with Asian themes when I had my birthday party.

Most children on their own have only a vague awareness of any barriers between cultures. While cultural misappropriation or disrespecting the symbols of one another's heritage is of real concern and requires attentive listening and action among adults, I think it is possible for children to gain greater understanding of the world through innocent cross-cultural play. A child can learn appreciation for cultural differences and develop easy, empathetic reflexes with others simply by playing. I didn't know I was pretending to be a different ethnicity, I was simply enjoying the novelty of tasty and pretty things that were different from my normal childhood experiences.

Who we become and what we want from life are shaped in different ways by what we learn as we develop toward adulthood. I clearly remember the inclusive sense of love I felt for humanity and the wish I made that day, leaning over the cake and blowing out those six candles in one breath. "I wish I could fly! I wish all the world knew God's love!" I decided that day my birthday wish was a keeper. I wished it over and over as I grew up and it still floats through my mind whenever I blow out birthday candles. My joy and conviction from those times on the swing set, having my hair washed at the kitchen sink, and playing with friends still continue to influence my perceptions and desires today.

Consequences

Theme: Battling and Bridging

"What? Where did this come from? You girls stole all this? What in the world were you thinking?"

My mom had come into our bedroom to put away some laundry and found my sister, Linda, and me counting out booty, an impressive pile of foreign currency and coins.

"No, Mommy, this doesn't belong to anybody. It's ours. We found it in the alley!"

Linda and I had been certain we had discovered real-life treasure. But just the tone of my mother's voice made my heart sink, my mood change, and caused me to realize in a flash that instead of having a grand escapade, we had stolen what didn't belong to us. It was my mother's reaction that completed the circuit in my brain. I suddenly recognized this might be a new version of the Pez Incident.

When we moved to a California ranch house in Pasadena, our play space opened up. Our backyard was large and the dirt alley behind held all kinds of things to be explored. My 5-year-old sister Linda and 7-year-old me thought a dilapidated and abandoned camper in the alley had adventure written all over it. We were sleuths like

Nancy Drew and we were in an adventure called The Mystery of the Old Trailer. There was certainly something suspicious inside, and we figured out how to open the lock with one of Dad's screwdrivers. Sneaking in, instead of a crime scene, we found a large drawer full of European money. We were rich! We were impressed with our spying skills, and until Mom came into our bedroom, we had also been delighted with our exotic-looking treasure.

My heart sank further when our mom sat down on the bed with us and explained we would have to return everything and apologize to our neighbors. Yes, the camper wasn't inside anyone's fence, but it was on the neighbor's property.

"Mommy, can't *you* just give it all back? We're sorry! Don't make us talk to them! Don't make us go over there!"

The answer was simple and firm, "No, you're the ones who took what wasn't yours, so you're the only ones who can make it right. You need to return everything you took, and you need to tell them you're sorry and won't do it again."

Children need patient and loving help from adults to understand the nuances of good behavior. Those who don't receive loving attention and get good supervision when they're young may end up being those who need correction from the courts when they're older. Children aren't born knowing all the applications of their culture's moral code. They can rarely answer in the moment when a frustrated adult asks, "What were you thinking?" But adults can help the child process the reasoning and feelings that went into a bad choice. They can help the child understand what they were thinking, where they went wrong, and how to develop strength of character.

Somehow I had figured out on my own that I didn't want to take what wasn't mine during the Pez Incident. Yet, I was able to commit grand larceny against my neighbor without a twinge of conscience until held to account by my mother. With my personality, and at that age, I didn't require a severe punishment to awaken my conscience. All it took was the disappointment in my mother's voice. Additionally, Mom taught us the consequence of stealing by making us confess our "trespass" and make it right.

Linda and I walked around the block, holding our treasure in front of us like thieves in shackles and rang the neighbor's doorbell. We told the grandmotherly woman who came to the door what we had done, said we were sorry and wouldn't take anything again. She was forgiving but stern. She repeated the moral lesson by strictly emphasizing we had done wrong by breaking into her trailer.

For my sister and me, our sense of humiliation and embarrassment and her unyielding attitude was enough of a punishment to scare us mostly straight. Becoming a moral individual and good citizen is something that's best cultivated within the context of simple community agreement about the standards. This neighbor we didn't know validated our mother's position.

To live well with each other, it's not just children who need to mature regarding the reasoning of why they make choices that go badly for themselves and others. All of us would do well to remain teachable about how our behavior impacts those around us and creates or diminishes our communal resilience. We all need to keep learning and adjusting our understanding. Ultimately, it's not the law that makes for a strong civil society, but all of us realizing that we must continue to work together to create it.

Wanna Race?

Second grade would never be the same. When I found out Julie would be moving to Los Gatos, I was certain fun times were over. Julie and I had a bigger and better imaginary world together than either of us had on our own. I missed her so much that school felt empty and lonely in spite of having other friends. Soon, though, I began to get to know a new girl in my class, Debbie Lee. Our friendship grew, and after a while fully occupied my attention. We were practically inseparable. We have continued to be fast friends for over fifty years now.

Recently, during lunch together at a local restaurant with two of our other childhood friends, Debbie told the story of how she felt about moving to town and starting school with us when she didn't know anybody. Debbie recounted to the others how I took pity on the scared and lonely Chinese American girl. I don't remember it that way. First of all, I didn't notice we were different in any discernible way. Secondly, I thought we were a lot alike. I felt sad and needed a new friend, and so did she. A big plus in this equation was that Debbie was willing to play whatever I cooked up. The playground games fueled by our imaginations continued in fresh ways for a year or two, until we eventually moved on to the fun of four-square matches, kickball, and other sports.

As the four of us old friends kept enjoying our lunch, a good chunk of our time was spent reminiscing about school days, unusual for us since we usually just catch up on the current events in our lives. We continued through that lunch hour on the topic of childhood, specifically talking about racial awareness, sharing our stories. I recall Natalie related one incident about how she and her two sisters were walking together to our school one morning. Their route took them past Washington Junior High School, where some students started maliciously yelling and jeering at the three sisters from the playground.

Natalie had expressed her hurt feelings at the verbal attack, expecting her sisters to agree, "I don't like black kids! They're mean!"

"And what do you think you are, Natalie? White? You're black, little sister. You're one of them. One of us! We're all black."

Natalie says the first time she had noticed skin color was a few years before when a boy in our first grade class called her the n-word. She remembers feeling surprised and hurt that a classmate was being mean to her. Angry, she talked after school with her sisters who explained the word and told her he was probably repeating what he heard from the adults at home. That incident left Natalie with both a sense of sadness as well as feelings of gratitude for the loving support she had in her family.

Yet, somehow when Natalie was walking by the yelling junior high kids bullying her and her sisters, their skin color had simply stood out—apart from her own—as a defining characteristic. It puzzled her. Perhaps she had subconsciously absorbed the predominant white culture's stereotypes.

Lorraine grew up largely unaware of race. To most kids, race is something you run, not something you are. Her father was an African American soldier stationed in Japan, who moved back to the states in the fifties with his Japanese wife. After Lorraine's younger siblings were born, when Lorraine was only 7, her father died of lung cancer. Lorraine's mother was left to raise three children alone. Lorraine's stories focused on her neighborhood in Altadena, her friendships at school, and the adults who played significant roles in her life.

We four discussed with gratitude the opportunities we had to form diverse friendships when we were little and the hurtful ways each of us began discovering as children how some people are hateful when it comes to differences. We talked about the particular ways we each learned that people of any color can be mean and get perverse pleasure out of making other people feel bad.

As we were growing up together in Southern California, one perspective we discovered we all shared was that we don't really know anything about people based on their appearance but on their character and their actions. After that day, I think we all felt a sense of renewed joy in being old friends who got to know each other before we understood that the world could be color coded. Having a wealth of these kinds of friendships weaves a rich tapestry of community strength.

Show and Tell

"What's your name, Robert? Robert! What's your name?" My girlfriend's dad, Dr. Dan Lee, was shouting from the driver's seat loud enough so all of us kids could hear.

I was sitting in the back of their Volkswagen camper van with Debbie, headed to Sunday services with her family after a sleepover the night before. Rob yelled from farther back where he sat with his younger sisters, Diana and Donna, "Di-dah-dit! Dah-dah-dah! Dah-di-di-dit!" Rob kept on shouting dots and dashes until he finished spelling his name in Morse code.

Dr. Lee had needed this skill as an 18-year-old when he escaped from Shanghai, China, just before it fell to communist forces. The ship he was on hit stormy seas, broke down and was in danger of foundering. Dan saved the day with his knowledge of both Morse code and English, helping the radio operator and captain solicit aid from a British destroyer that towed them to Taiwan. Traveling with a buddy, Dan, and his German shepherd made the newspaper as he toured the island on the Harley Davidson he had brought with him on the ship. His father had happily agreed to give Dan the bike as a victory prize, thinking he would never be able to win the national amateur boxing championship of China with his small amount of training. Knowing a motorcycle hung in the balance, Dan was motivated to win his fights and became the national champ.

I was reminded at Dr. Lee's funeral in 2015 how readily children accept the eccentricities of the adults in their lives as common or normal, construing their own internal stories to accommodate information. During the service, Debbie, Rob, some of Dr. Lee's Tai Chi Chuan students, Jeet Kun Do friends and Linda Lee Cadwell, the widow of martial arts expert Bruce Lee, shared different stories that brought back many fun and nostalgic memories of growing up with Dan Lee as one of the fathers in my life.

My impression of him as a child was that he was something like an incognito superhero. He was a NASA scientist with lots of technology in his study, had useful gadgets he invented, told stories about his daring escape from China that included being shot at, and he knew Chinese, Morse code, and English. Also, his friendship and training sessions with Bruce Lee (whom I knew as Kato from Batman and The Green Hornet), sealed the deal. Debbie's dad put the polish on my childish affection and admiration for him by performing really convincing magic tricks at her birthday parties.

I remember Dr. Lee's sense of humor and learning from him that Chinese was written in rows that ran up and down rather than across the page. He would say it was how he was able to read a little Chinese New Testament he had been given on the ship as it lurched up and down over rough seas. He comically demonstrated how he would hold the book steady as his body rose and fell with the waves and his eyes tracked the columns of characters.

As children, one of the ways we discover what the world is and how it works is from the many adults who populate our lives. The shape of the world we perceive and what we believe to be true about it by the time we ourselves are adults is in part the product of our unique encounters and interpretations. It's one reason we can be so different even from our siblings who share so much of our background.

From the time I was 7, next to my own family, I spent most of my time with Debbie's, accepting any differences between our two families as unimpressive because, from my perspective, we had almost everything in common. Both of our fathers worked at Jet Propulsion Laboratory, and our mothers stayed home. We kids all went to the same elementary school. Both of our families had a VW bus and a VW bug. We went to the same church and our parents were in the same Sunday school class, attending most of the same events and parties. Deb and I were both the oldest in our families. Since her parents came from different parts of China—her dad spoke Mandarin and her mom, Cantonese—everyone spoke English at her house just as we did at mine.

While her mom used a wok and a rice cooker, two things we didn't have at the time in our kitchen, my mom used an aebleskiver pan to make traditional Danish ball-shaped pancakes, a unique menu item among my friends. Her dad spent time in his study with radios and audio equipment and in a darkroom developing his photos. My dad spent time building a rec room for a ping-pong table in the backyard and adding an extra bedroom on to our house.

The differences between Debbie and me seemed unimportant as we were growing up, yet we were each experiencing the world from our own perspectives, in spite of everything we had in common, shaped by the larger society around us. I think we both were benefitting from our friendship, maturing in our understanding of cultures because we were learning unconsciously, each from the other, and from the time spent with our families.

We both remember singing a song in our second-grade Sunday school class, though our memories diverge over how it felt. I recall feeling joy as my attention was drawn to various skin colors as though we were describing flavors of candy. Debbie recalls feeling discomfort, something I failed to notice at the time, because she would be selected and singled out to be one of the children up front as part of the visual aid for yellow in the song's words:

"Jesus loves the little children, all the children of the world. Red and yellow, black and white, they are precious in his sight. Jesus loves the little children of the world."

I can still feel my childhood joy as I type those words. The song reminds me now of Martin Luther King Jr.'s dream imagery of children of different colors joining hands as sisters and brothers. But I think it's important to recognize, I could afford to simply find the song a description of the colors God uses to paint the world. I didn't carry the same burden or face the same biases Debbie and her family did, which came as a result of being immigrants and looking different from the majority of people in our community. I could afford to be colorblind, but that wasn't a luxury that served them well, as prejudice shaped their experiences and restricted their inclusion and opportunities.

I don't recall noticing the Lee family was different in any significant way from the Burden family until we had been friends for years. Debbie seemed to be embarrassed when her grandmother came up to the front of the school auditorium after a performance to congratulate Debbie in Chinese and give her a traditional, celebratory red envelope with money in it. I gave some thought to why getting money from her grandmother felt difficult for Deb. I was old enough at the time to recognize that becoming the focus of attention for being different in a group of kids is rarely pleasant.

Years later, Debbie became a second-grade teacher in Arcadia, a neighboring town, after she and her husband spent time teaching in the Marshall Islands. One year, when Debbie was doing a unit titled Friendship, she called to see if I was willing to be her Show and Tell for the day. She was teaching her students the importance of working to make friends and wanted them to understand that friendships made in second grade could be nurtured into adulthood.

I really enjoyed myself as we shared some stories of how our friendship formed, different fun things we had done together over the years, and ways we had helped each other. At one point, her students, sitting on the floor as I sat on a chair to read a book to them, became fixated on my penny loafers.

"Ms. Cox, are you wearing man shoes?"

I explained that they were women's shoes, but that the style was something worn by men and women, kind of like tennis shoes. Another child told me their mommy always wore high heels, and I said, that for me, it was better I wore flats. As the class examined my footwear at their eye level, they became excited to see that I had a penny in each shoe. I explained how penny loafers had been popular since my parents were young. Their assumptions about the antiquity of my shoes, since my parents wore them before me, gave us a laugh. We had to make a concerted effort to get the discussion about the importance of friendship back on track.

Overall, I think we were a good visual for Debbie's students, who live in the Arcadia School District, where the majority ethnic group is Asian. Giving younger generations and more recent immigrants insight into the beauty of making friends across our artificial lines of division is important.

Schools are the obvious places for young people to learn how to get along, but there are many other places and opportunities where we can draw attention to friendships that are working if we adults recognize there may be value in allowing a childlike Show-and-Tell attitude to be a part of our culture. Rather than pretending to be color-blind, let's consider being more open in sharing our insights and talking in relaxed ways about what's delightful in our differences and cross-cultural experiences. Where it's possible, let's invite the kind of dialogue that will help us add to our positive experiences and broaden our understanding about apparent differences, friendships and possibilities. Something this simple really can move us toward becoming a more united and resilient nation.

Amazing Grace

"Good morning to you! Good morning to you! We're all in our places with bright shining faces! Oh, this is the way, to start a new day!"

Mom sang her way into our bedrooms in the morning, the smell of perking coffee wafting in her wake, pulling up blinds, opening curtains, letting us know it was time to rise and shine. She was a singer. Not that we always appreciated that first thing on a Monday morning. When she was a girl, she and Aunt Lois would be called upon to sing duets at their small Baptist church, but Mom didn't contribute her voice to our Congregational church choir when we were kids. She just sang the musical soundtrack of our lives at home, permanently tuned to hymns and worship songs, with the occasional love song from the 1950s thrown in. Our mother's voice hardwired us to believe God was good, full of grace, forgiveness and fresh starts.

In trouble? Sinking down? Over your head? Need a friend? Love is present to help. Lost? Blind? A wretch like me? There's grace. I grew up knowing that the limited love my family or others had to offer was not the final word. There was hope beyond any circumstance. The bottom line was amazing grace.

Not everyone finds comfort in a larger spiritual story, and religion can certainly be used to twist these very themes. But in my life, the lyrics of those gospel songs from childhood really were "good news." They contained the assurance that there was always unconditional love present and available, whether I could see it or not. There was a rock-solid stability in our love story.

But life is never some picture-perfect, solve-it-in-an-episode, consistent existence. All of us fail to receive the fullness of the love our souls seem to need to feel perpetually free and self-actualized. Many in my circles of family and friendship have suffered extreme loss and disillusionment. Most of us have felt enough pain, turmoil and confusion to at least question the existence of a "true north" love that makes sense of a world rife with war, hunger and disease. For me, there was a gradual dawning awareness of inconsistencies.

One evening, stunned by something my grandmother had casually observed, I left the kitchen, walking through the house, and stepped down into the quiet sanctuary of my bedroom, a converted glass porch, covered in shade and scent in the evenings from our mock orange trees. Sitting at the old dressing table Mom had recently refurbished, I held up my hands next to my head, fanning them to block my view of straight blond hair as I stared into the shadows in my mirror. I was looking for a truth, too big and too painful for my 7-year-old self. I felt as though the ground, my foundation of security, was slipping out from around my feet the way the ocean would pull away the sand when I stood in the shallows, watching the waves crash by.

I had come in from school, excited to show my grand-mother my second-grade class pictures. She had expressed surprise at the appearance of a classmate I thought was beautiful, pointing and referring to my black girlfriend as a "little pickaninny," a term I didn't know. It was her dismissive tone of voice that felt like a blow to my heart. I didn't understand, and I made an excuse to go to my room to nurse my hurt and try to make sense of what she had said.

Staring into the mirror at my reflection, I remember trying to assimilate a new, profound thought, "If I looked different... if my hair was brown and in braids... would Grandma know me? If I didn't look like me, would Grandma be able to see I belonged to her? What would it be like if I was the same person on the inside but didn't look like me on the outside?"

I didn't know my grandmother was using a racial slur. I didn't know the word, though I learned the sound of discrimination and prejudice that day. I understood my Grandma's tone of voice. She considered my girlfriend to be less than me because of the way she looked. At the time, I thought she was referencing something about the difference in our hair.

I think I remember this moment as clearly as I do because, in contrast, my grandmother was so kindly indulgent of me. I hadn't known her to be harsh or sharp-tongued. As an adult, I'm able to look back on how hard her life had been on an isolated farm in Kansas, responsible for younger siblings, with little education and almost no exposure to anyone other than her family. My grandmother was born in an era when women's voices were not heard and they had no vote. I can marvel now that she was generous to us with her time and efforts, given how little had been given to her.

I don't think I became racially conscious at that point when Grandma pointed out a difference that mattered to her. I don't recall noticing or determining who of my friends were white and who were not. But, I do think the hurt I felt was the beginning of recognizing there was something wrong in the world that felt shallow and uninformed by the depths of real love. If a grandmother could dismiss and not care about a child based on the way she looked in a picture, something wasn't right. I was beginning to discover that family love was not the strong thing I had thought it was. Even a grandmother's love could be fragile and weak. Real love doesn't disappear just because someone looks different.

"You need to give the guard your purse, honey, so he can look through it and make sure you're not bringing anything inside that's not allowed."

I lifted my little handbag up to the counter for the prison guard to look through. With heart pounding, I followed Daddy through the sally port and continued doing what we were instructed, as our prison escort led us to the inmate visiting room.

Starting when I was in third grade, our little family of five dressed up, went to our Sunday school and church services at Lake Avenue Congregational, and then drove to Terminal Island Federal Prison. I loved my Uncle Stan, my dad's tall and handsome kid brother. He moved through life with a swagger like James Dean, wearing jeans and a white t-shirt with a pack of cigarettes rolled up in his sleeve, exposing the military tattoo on his arm. It was confusing to think of him as a prisoner since only scary, bad grownups were put behind bars. On that first visit, I was trying to figure out if I would recognize him when I saw him. Had he changed into a kind of monster that needed to be placed in a cage? Would he be able to recognize me? Would he still love me if he had become bad and I was still good?

We were escorted into a bright room that seemed more like a cafeteria than a prison. Almost immediately, I recognized my uncle sitting at a table waiting for us, and ran to him. He stood up and swung me into his arms for a familiar hug and tobacco kiss. He put me back down and greeted the rest of the family. Mommy got us kids set up with coloring books and crayons while the grownups talked. As I looked around the visitor's room, I was surprised to see lots of prisoner daddies with mommies and kids. It was a puzzle. People in prison looked like people in my neighborhood and community. Bad men who had committed crimes and needed to be in jail, looked like daddies, uncles and grandfathers.

In the mind of a child with a third-grade understanding of math, things should be straightforward. One side is simply supposed to equal the other. My sister and I had taken something that didn't belong to us. We had committed a crime. We had been sorry for our actions and able to make things right. My uncle had illegal drugs he wasn't supposed to have and committed the same crime but would be away from us in prison for years. Was it because he wasn't sorry? Could he make things right somehow? If you were a grownup, could you be forgiven? Added to the ongoing confusion and contrast of Sundays spent at church and prison was the knowledge that my grandmother would only love me if I had my recognizable straight blond hair like the rest of the family, and not if my hair was brown and curly. Not only was love in question, my understanding of how faith intertwined with the law was being jostled.

The first inconsistencies were cracking reality with paradoxes. My well-ordered and predictable world was becoming more complex. Thankfully, it was happening in a home and community that emphasized grace: freely given and unearned love. As we grow up, we accommodate new and inconsistent information in different ways, trying to create sense and meaning from the things we experience.

Few of us are aware of the process as it's happening. We are mostly unconscious about the ways our understanding of the world and our place in it is being constructed. Even as adults, many of us remain ignorant about the unique lens we're viewing reality through. Recalling our childhood experiences, especially our first memories of how we became aware of volatile adult topics like race, religion, cultural and national identity and politics will give us more solid ground to meet on—together.

Stories From Africa

As I dusted carved wood elephants, giraffes, buffalo and antelope, our Aunt Dorothy, in a simple housedress, with her white hair in a regal bun, enthralled me with the suspenseful story of how she and Uncle George had first moved to Africa in 1943. Their belongings had traveled on a different ship from theirs and had gone to the bottom of the Atlantic, sunk by a German submarine. The young couple had arrived in Africa without any of the material goods and tools they had thought were absolutely necessary, to begin their work with the people living near Lake Victoria.

As my sisters and I were growing up in a mostly white Pasadena neighborhood in the 1960s and 1970s, we had the opportunity to share life with an unusually diverse group of friends. One of the ways that happened was through George and Dorothy Smoker, an older Mennonite couple who owned a house down the street from us and had spent much of their lives as missionaries in Africa. The two of them and many of their friends became an integral part of our lives. When Dad began an addition on our house, Uncle George came to pitch in with what building skills he had. In turn, Mom and we girls would help Aunt Dorothy with household chores at the two-story farmhouse that had been her childhood home and over time had become a part of our suburban neighborhood.

I remember Aunt Dorothy's self-deprecating humor as she related how she and George had gone to British East Africa, proud and sure of their missionary training to teach Africans. Over time, as they became acquainted with those they had come to Africa to teach, they grew to understand that they were the ones with more to learn about radical love, grace and forgiveness. We heard many stories from our adopted aunt and uncle about tribal conflicts with the Mau Maus and others, colonial injustice and learning to live together as brothers and sisters, even under harsh and hate-filled circumstances. Dorothy wrote books filled with interviews and oral histories from colonial and post-colonial Africa. In one book, *Ambushed By Love,* she described attacks, murders and immense suffering as well as the unprecedented forgiveness of one's enemies that went far beyond any open-hearted grace I've been able to live out. Dorothy and George and the echo of those stories continue to inspire and challenge me.

During their absences from our Pasadena neighborhood, when the Smokers were living and working in Africa, their two-story house became the temporary residence for a variety of short- and long-term visitors coming to Los Angeles for college, graduate studies or work at a local seminary. My parents always enjoyed making friends and invited these folks from Africa, Asia, South America, India, the Pacific Islands and Europe for meals or a place to stay when the house down the street was full. As a result, we were not only exposed to cultures completely different from ours but we had the joy of learning about a variety of traditions from people who cared about us and appreciated the differences between our perspectives.

Some of our family's most enjoyable times during those years were spent with the Africans. Many were living with very turbulent conditions and difficult circumstances in their home countries. Some were experiencing painful civil conflicts, and others the necessary upheaval that came with the end of colonialism and beginning of independence and self-governance. In spite of the hardships they had endured and would face when they returned to their countries, the people who came through our home had an overriding sense of optimism and enthusiasm for life.

Sharing meals together was especially fun and memorable. My mom enjoyed trying to replicate the food folks missed from home. One favorite and often-repeated meal with the Africans involved shaping thick cornmeal porridge into a small cup with one hand and using it to dip into a communal bowl of stew set in the middle of the table. As we ate, we would share stories. Our friends would describe their home countries. We learned the landscapes of their childhoods, their hopes for their communities and nations. We learned some of their customs and learned something of the heartaches, losses and challenges they faced. Mostly, though, I remember laughing.

We also heard more about our parents' lives than we would have without these guests. Mom and Dad would respond to these visitors around our table with stories of their own, about an earlier time in America, of lessons learned in the Depression, and the differences between their childhoods and ours. We heard about California during World War II, when German prisoners of war worked in neighborhood orange groves, of block wardens, victory gardens and childhood adventures. We kids were also included in the circle of conversation, asked about our day's happenings at school, about the sports we played, and our thoughts about current world events or our feelings about God. Unconsciously, my life was shaped as I came to value time spent with friends and family and grew to understand the importance of simply listening to one another's stories. I learned that spending time with people who are different in age, color and country from us expands our understanding of the world and the people in it.

Open Hands

Methuselah Nyagwaswa sat at our kitchen table, describing his dismay when he spotted the pride of lions. They were spread out, resting in the brush just off to his right as he found his way along the path in the twilight. He had known it was unwise to risk traveling through this valley, notorious for its many lions, but he had felt an urgency to get back to his village in time for his father's funeral. We kids sat, hardly breathing, as he told us how he had prayed before entering the valley, calling on the God who closed the lions' mouths for Daniel to do the same for him. We could see those Tanzanian lions in our minds' eyes, watching young Methuselah as he walked past them, protected by angels.

Through stories like this, I grew up knowing faith in God was tangible and practical. In addition to my parents, people like Methuselah taught us the importance of having the courage to persevere through difficulty for the sake of love, family and community.

In 1965, the year of the Watts riots in Los Angeles, our family became close friends with Methuselah when he moved into a converted upstairs apartment at the house down the street. The same age as our dad, Methuselah seemed younger and more playful to us kids than other adults. He went to school like we did and had the flexible hours of a graduate student. Often he told us stories about his childhood, describing an adventurous rural life in a beautiful country that contrasted with our own urban experiences in smog-choked Southern California before emission laws gave us back the views of the San Gabriel Mountains. Eventually he met a nurse, Josephine, from Kenya, fell in love and asked her to marry him. Dad and Mom were the best man and matron of honor at their wedding, and their reception was held in our backyard.

I recall a story he once told us and the natural sense of empathy and connection I felt with little 7-year-old Methuselah, who wanted to learn how to read and write. To get an education, he had to leave his village to find a missionary boarding school his family had heard about that was far from their home. Walking into the compound to begin classes was the first time he had ever seen white people. I imagined being in his situation, far from home, and seeing people with skin different from mine for the very first time.

One of the most important things I learned from Methuselah in the years he was our neighbor was his genuine practice of forgiveness, which, unfortunately, he needed on many occasions, being subjected to prejudice and disdain simply by going about normal, daily life as a black man.

One day, Mom drove Methuselah to the barbershop for a haircut and accompanied him inside. The barber turned from his customer in the chair and said he couldn't do "hair like his," indicating Methuselah with a lift of his chin. Mom, being naïve at this point about prejudice, had responded practically, telling the barber that it was simple with electric clippers and it was really no different from a crew cut on straight hair. The barber had insisted that he didn't do "hair like his" and told Mom to take him to the other side of town. Mom and Methuselah turned and left the shop, with Mom angry and offended. Standing out on the sidewalk together, Methuselah raised his eyebrows at Mom and said with a smile, "Well, sister, let's find that other barbershop."

At the car, when Mom questioned him about why he wasn't angry, hurt and offended by the barber's treatment, Methuselah responded by holding his hands open in front of him, palms up, saying, "When others give me their words, I don't need to keep them all. I can hold them with open hands and ask God to take from me the ones that will not help me and leave only the ones that will." Methuselah forgave the barber and gave his words no power. The image of Methuselah's peaceful, openhanded rejection of bitter words has been a valuable and challenging example for me. As a child, I took these kinds of lessons to heart because they came from an adult whose joyful love for others was apparent.

After his studies in America, Methuselah went back home to develop the English curriculum for Tanzania, putting to use the education he gained here and leaving us with the lessons of character he brought with him from Africa. I was fortunate to have a variety of people in my life who challenged my thinking and stretched my heart. The people we share our lives with influence and shape us and contribute to our moral character in the same way Methuselah powerfully and unintentionally taught our family about the beauty of forgiveness.

Our relationships are a form of education, just as the people and characters who inhabit what we listen to and see in the media are. We continue to learn and be influenced by the people sharing our lives and filling our imaginations. If we choose to, we can all use this opportunity for ourselves and for our children by populating our lives with people of nobility of thought, wisdom, good humor and compassion.

True Americans

I had just turned ten when Martin Luther King Jr. was shot in Memphis, Tennessee. I don't have a memory of the news coverage or of talking about his death with my parents. What I do remember clearly is, a week or so after his assassination, stumbling out of Pasadena Christian School's auditorium with tears in my eyes after seeing a news documentary on the Civil Rights Era.

Even now, decades later, I can still replay some of the images in my mind's eye like a traumatic event or recurring nightmare. In the grainy, black-and-white footage, a nighttime scene unfolded. Lit by truck headlights, men with their backs to the camera, dressed in hooded white "choir robes," stood outside a small white bungalow that looked similar to the house across the street from my family's home. I watched as a few men struggled together to raise a heavy cross, the scene reminding me of the picture my dad had shown me of his fellow Marines raising the flag on Iwo Jima.

I remember a 10-year-old's feelings of being plunged into the visual stories of the Civil Rights Movement that day, trying to make sense of the footage I was being shown. I had no context except my own childhood in Los

Angeles, surrounded by diverse and loving adults. The documentary's narrator was describing exclusion, prejudice and hate in an America I couldn't recognize. I grew up completely believing in a beautiful country, one that stood in stark contrast to the realities I was seeing on the screen. As the swirl of new information continued, I was in shock, still attempting to make sense of why a men's choir, or maybe monks, would go out in the night with their faces hidden by hoods to set Jesus' cross on fire. As the visual evidence grew of white grownups in America acting hatefully, I was grieved and sickened.

In 1968, there were limited ways for a child to see national news, and I had missed these scenes of the Civil Rights Era as they unfolded. That day I was barraged with the black-and-white facts of our nation's hardness of heart: of police hitting women with nightsticks, clubbing them to the ground as those women walked peacefully in their Sunday best, unarmed across a bridge; of firemen using high-pressure hoses on children, ripping through their clothing, knocking them over; of police dogs being set on mothers and fathers; and of white adults attacking students both black and white from behind as they sat together at a restaurant counter.

Being young, I had only a dim awareness of any of these events taking place from a few adult conversations I had overheard. There are many different ways a child's innocence can be stolen. Many children suffer its loss earlier than ten and less benignly than watching a movie. For me, the discovery from this film that showed my heroes—firemen and police officers—behaving like criminals, unsettled everything.

I was completely unprepared to see cowardly American men acting violently toward other Americans, especially nonviolent women and children. I had no ability to determine that my place in the story, based on the color of my skin or that of my family's, was with the white authority figures. My child sight gave me a very simple, clear-eyed view of the kind of behavior I was witnessing in the newsreel: men who represented American law and order were behaving viciously, without compassion or even common sense. None of the people I saw being attacked, hurt and carried away by the officials were behaving like criminals.

The actions of these uniformed men flew in the face of everything I was learning at school and was being taught at home. The leaders who were shown standing on stairs or surrounded by reporters holding microphones or in front of symbols of power and authority seemed small-minded and ridiculous. Hate made the biggest men appear shriveled and anemic. In the position of police chief, mayor or governor, they spouted impotent words that made no sense in light of what I believed about the United States of America.

In elementary school, day after day the true standard for our nation was raised in my mind when my schoolmates and I declared in unison, "I pledge allegiance to the flag of the United States of America, and to the Republic for which it stands, one nation under God, indivisible, with liberty and justice for *all*."

I wonder how many people living in the United States right now have taken the time to watch Civil Rights footage like the documentary I saw. It would do us all good to revert to a simple child-like perspective and pull up videos of the marches from Selma to Montgomery, of news footage of lunch counter protests and the attacks on the Freedom Riders. You need to see for yourself the contradictions with the simplest tenets of our national identity.

I've had friends say, "That was a long time ago and things are different now." However, we're still honoring those who promoted the counterfeit American ideals of superiority and privilege with plaques, statues and schools named after those forgers. To this day, the bridge in Alabama where peaceful protestors were attacked and beaten by the police remains named for a member of the Ku Klux Klan. We do not want to condone these acts of unjustified violence and cruelty by elevating those who promoted hatred. We need to understand the cautionary tales in our history and honor those who suffered and those who sacrificed while seeking justice. In whose footsteps do we want our children following? It is crucial to our resilience as a nation to hold up as a standard those people who practice great courage, compassion, liberty and peace.

Where Stories
Intersect

Hearts racing, my little sisters and I looked up, startled by the pounding on the front door, the quiet of the house shattered. It was a summer morning and we had been playing in our bedrooms as my mom finished the breakfast dishes. Mom went to the front door and the pounding was replaced with a woman's angry shouting, her voice raised in accusation, "You stole my baby! You can't have her! She's mine!"

I was 9 when my sweet, 7-month-old, towheaded cousin came to live with us. Her father, Stan, my dad's brother, was in prison for selling heroin, and her mother, Cecelia, was afflicted by her own demons. Karla's crib was put in my room and her baby chortles became my morning alarm clock. We three girls welcomed this new, ready-made sister. She was one of us four. In old pictures we look like color-coordinated goofballs, stair-stepping down, dressed in outfits from Mom's busy sewing machine.

In hindsight, it would have been simpler if my parents had legally adopted Karla, but that would have meant getting the law involved in our family business. At the time, no one saw that as a kind or straightforward solution.

My aunt shoved her way into the house that morning, under the influence and swinging away like an erratic boxer. Mom, who was trying to stop her, was yelling, "Stop! Get out of here! You know you're in no condition to take care of her! Go home and sleep!"

We four girls watched from the hallway as the shoving continued. My aunt jostled Mom out of the way and came toward us. Scared and frozen in place, we were completely unprepared for any kind of conflict. Mom yelled, "Diane, get the girls! Run! Lock the door!"

We turned and ran. Carrying Karla, pushing the two others in front of me, I locked us into the back bedroom. Our mothers continued to fight, coming down the long hallway as Mom threatened to call the police, picking up the receiver, only to have my aunt knock it out of her hand.

That morning we didn't need the police to restore peace, although there were other times we did. Our aunt's anger unexpectedly dissolved into tears of defeated self-pity. Mom persuaded her to go into the living room where she promptly fell asleep on the sofa. Hours later, when she woke in a better state of mind, she took Karla back to her apartment for the weekend. Karla continued to live with us, except for random weekends, until she was 10 and her mother took her full time.

The sense or meaning the adults in our family were able to make of the different crazy happenings in those years as they all talked, processed and reached understanding together, didn't always trickle down to us children. While we continued to interact and talk easily as a family about typical topics like schoolwork and friends, there was also a new kind of accepted chaos and turmoil that was impacting all of us, yet rarely came with formal explanations.

It's almost impossible for even the most functional adults to offer children all the age-appropriate guidance about the meaning of complex issues and events that impact their lives. Many people assume that children, in their innocence, aren't noticing or being affected by what's troubling the adults, but children's development can be shaped by these events. Topics like addiction, mental illness, driving under the influence, financial crisis, homelessness, skid row and the role of police, courts, social workers and foster care systems become relevant to many families. Often not acknowledged, these things can live in the shadows, around the edges of our more routine lives.

Years later, Karla, now an adult, walked into the community center in Northern California for a memorial gathering for our Aunt Wanda. It was one of the first times our extended family had been together in years. Family members of all ages warmly greeted Karla as she came through the door, glad to see her and welcome her back into the larger circle of love.

It had been 31 years since Karla left our home. We had been blindly assured all those years before that everything would be good for her in that arrangement. After all, the reasoning went, children belong with their mothers. Still, we girls grieved her absence from our circle of sisters.

After Karla's move "home" we had seen very little of her. We missed her but assumed as the years went by, that we were all simply occupied with the fast pace of life. On rare occasions, Karla and her mother would stop by for a short visit on a holiday. Looking back, it's easy to recognize we had amiable but emotionally distant relationships.

As it turned out, whatever emptiness and hurt we felt in losing our little sister was nothing compared to the sense of abandonment and confusion Karla experienced. Up until then, she had only spent time with her family of origin as an occasional weekend visitor. At ten, she wasn't equipped for the many challenges she faced by moving home. Her mother regularly told Karla she was no longer wanted because she was a difficult and disobedient child. Too young to recognize the lies and manipulation, she believed she couldn't appeal to the other adults in the family to make things right again.

By sixteen, tired of the chaos and unknown to the rest of the family, she moved out, making do, living with friends or on her own when she could afford it. She was convinced by the years of lies that she was troublesome and unwelcome. It wasn't until she walked into the community center and was welcomed by one relative after another that she realized the family love she'd known as a child still existed. It's been a process for all of us. It takes time to sort truth from lies. Karla's journey has been arduous and brave. She's brought a refreshing and humorous perspective, particular strength, and hard-won wisdom with her return to our family.

When it comes to resilience, most of us grow up learning survival skills. Thriving skills are harder to come by. It's just common sense that we are all better off when we're each willing to keep growing and maturing long after we're old enough to vote. Becoming fully compassionate human beings is a journey of many miles, elevation changes, and innumerable twists and turns. However, not everyone stays teachable and open to their continuing growth and evolution. The issues facing our world take more maturity and wisdom than any of us have naturally. We all need to do the hard work of seeking what's true and being willing to learn, grow and develop.

Where Stories
Contradict

"That never happened. You're making that up!"

I had just picked some lemons and was telling my friend Nancy about the hot days when I was a kid doing yard work with my family. My mom would pick lemons from our tree, go in the house for a while, and emerge with icy glasses of the best-tasting, freshly made lemonade. Nancy surprised me by reacting with anger and said I was making it all up. She felt I was being overly sentimental. To Nancy, having a mother who makes and serves lemonade and a father who shares easy camaraderie with his children was the stuff of scripted, 1950s television shows like *Leave It To Beaver* and *Father Knows Best*.

Nancy grew up in what was called the Big House in the 1950s and 1960s, a nine-bedroom home in Oregon her mother bought when she saw a business opportunity. The prostitutes Nancy's mom knew had no one to watch their children when they were working, so she bought the large place to offer these mothers boarding with childcare and meals. She had strict standards; no "Johns" were allowed at the house.

Nancy's mother was a strong woman with an attitude that claimed that pulling oneself up by the bootstraps was entirely possible, whatever the circumstances. She was also smart and savvy, seeing how some women needed help with childcare. Nancy says what compassion her mother had came from strength, not empathy. If anyone were to express how hard something was, she'd tell them they didn't need to feel sorry for themselves. She was unlikely to deal kindly with a woman she considered weak and needy, but if a woman was trying to do something for herself and her children, she'd go out of her way to help them.

Nancy and I met in the early '80s at a home Bible study. She was a hairstylist and a single mother doing her best to raise her two boys with more love and wisdom than she was given when she was growing up. Her childhood was filled with much harsher circumstances than mine. Still, it wasn't until she was an adult, telling friends about her life as a kid and they said it was an excruciating story that she paused to consider if that was true.

Nancy is an optimist, the strong, no-nonsense woman her mother raised her to be. Only in recent years has Nancy been able to recognize how lonely she felt as a child and also how much her mother loved her. She doesn't so much feel her childhood was unbearably painful as it was challenging and character-building.

As we got to know each other, it took a lot of back and forth for us to understand where the other was coming from. Our households were extremely different during our formative years. Almost every time we talked I learned something profound from her journey. She and I saw the world through completely different lenses, and yet much of the time we shared the joy of simply "getting" each other. Ultimately, both of our viewpoints on the world were expanded by our friendship as we wrestled together over difficult topics and our individual understandings, coming as we were from different life experiences.

Nancy and others have helped me unearth more of my heart; to recognize that my childhood needs a deeper look to make it and the characters in it entirely human and the events less idyllic or horrifying, as the case may be.

For reasons that run the gamut, most of us need to reexamine our memories as children if we're going to benefit from the hidden wisdom in our own stories. It's easy to be absolutely convinced by our false narratives, those interpretations of our lives that only serve our personal agendas. We can pick and choose the way we tell our stories to boost our ego, buffer our pain or rationalize our purely self-serving motives.

It took my friend Sheri to point out that I was being inconsistent when I talked about my high school experiences. Sometimes I said it was a favorite time in my life. At other times, I said it was traumatic. It turned out both were true, but it took some processing to make sense of how that could be. Where there is pain, there is often opportunity for living deeper.

My friend Mary shared a metaphor some years ago when friends were trying to sort out the good and the bad in the way they had been raised. She said that ultimately, what we initially believe about our lives is just a flimsy house of cards. Rather than trying to carefully pull one card or another out from our construction to try to fix that one little piece, it's better to let the whole thing fall down so we can start over. Perfect love doesn't look like anything we know yet. We need to keep a learner's mind and seek the fresh designs that best fit the seasons and challenges we're living in.

As I learned from Nancy, it's not always easy to relate to one another's perspectives. The lenses we've received from our families or the ones we've formed through persuasive experiences are often so convincing and have become so much a part of us that we unwittingly believe we can flawlessly see the world through them. It's hard to imagine how it's even possible for the same facts to look completely different when viewed from a different angle but it is. If we determine we can and will respectfully discuss our differing points of view, we'll be able to move toward decisions that are mutually beneficial and increase communal stability.

Leadership

We never talk about the world outside—things like politics, religion, work or money—when we hang out with family at a cabin in Oregon. It's a rule laid down long before our family of five ever got to share some of the days my sister-in-law, Susan's family enjoys on the lake each summer. Her husband, Tom, has been spending time in the rustic old place since he was 2 years old and the original owner, Wally, invited Tom's parents and other friends with young families to round out his life as a single guy. Wally liked the privacy of his room overlooking the lake but loved having his self-made family of noisy, happy adults and kids around him during the day, at the dinner table and by the campfire at night.

Wally's gone now, but the traditions continue. Tom, who is a judge in Alaska, was reminiscing during the summer of 2017 about how the cabin has always been a no-conflict zone. Whatever is going on "out there" doesn't flavor the conversations or influence the time together at the lake. It's a world to itself. He said kindness and good humor have always prevailed.

But, a couple nights later, for just a few minutes, the traditional rule of order broke down a bit. While we sat around after dinner, the talk turned to the concerns we have regarding Americans who continue to emphasize our differences and intensify our divisions. A few mentioned the combative and antagonistic words being spoken and the matter-of-fact acceptance of war as an option, including the potential use of nuclear weapons.

Tom mused that when he was a teenager growing up in the 1960s he had assumed our generation of Baby Boomers would produce a different breed of politicians and business people that would work for the common good and seek ways to pursue peace. Tom prioritizes those values in his courtroom. For a while, we processed together what seems to be the loss of influence from those who experienced the trauma of the Vietnam War firsthand, and others, like us who grew up horrified by images of the war being broadcast into our living rooms. Why have we allowed so many of our representatives and the businesses that serve us to promote special interests instead of our best intentions as a peaceful nation?

Because of the rest and relaxation rule at the cabin, it wasn't long before our conversation flowed away from political references toward ways of continuing to participate in positive change. But, even though we moved on that night, those thoughts kept echoing in my head over the next days. For some reason an "earworm" of a jingle popped in as well, "I'd like to teach the world to sing in perfect harmony," from a 1971 soda pop commercial. I like how songs sometimes float up from our unconscious and fill in the gaps of what we're feeling. It's oversimplified but still, if only we could just share a drink and a song, maybe we could create a little harmony.

"What doesn't kill you makes you stronger!"

The crowd was excited, jumping up and down and waving their arms in sync. Their enthusiasm was contagious and I got to my feet, caught up in the moment. I sang along as Kelly Clarkson and our friends, Jill and Kate, her backup singers at the time, belted out the lyrics as though they had freshly discovered every word to be true.

I appreciate artists who write from their own stories and present something of their journey through music. When authentic emotion and personal discovery are shared, a kind of catharsis can take place for the people listening. *Stronger* felt exactly like that, liberating. My spirits were lifted as I joined in, helping me get rid of mental images of disaster and replacing them with ones from a crowd jubilantly affirming strength and resilience.

When we were working on Hurricane Irene in Albany in 2012, our friend Jason, Kelly's music director, invited us to a concert down at Bethel Woods Entertainment complex where the historic Rock Music and Art Festival took place in New York during August of 1969. Hanging out on the tour bus with him after the show, we all talked about the implications of Woodstock and other events in the '60s based on what Graeme and I had seen in the museum earlier that evening.

Jason hadn't even been born in 1969, but Graeme and I were 11 the summer of Woodstock. The impression the two of us had at the time was of a crazy, psychedelic drug orgy in the mud, all set to music. We don't recall giving it much thought after that. Neither of us was much into rock music at that age, drugs were of no importance and the thought of orgies was gross. In the Los Angeles news cycle, if we even saw it, Woodstock was just one more news blip on our small black and white televisions, taking a back seat to the ongoing war in Vietnam and the gruesome Tate murders that had happened the week before. My main interest in August of 1969 was making the most of summer vacation with weekdays spent at the Caltech pool and fun on the weekends with family and friends at local beaches. To 11-year-olds, history-making hippies were of little interest.

So, touring the museum at Bethel Woods had given us a larger historical context to the event. The exhibit described the festival's evolution from a hopeful, profit-making, music and art venture that might draw several thousand attendees at most, into an expression of peaceful protest that attracted over 400,000. Because of the overwhelming number of people showing up, the organizers gave up charging admission and it turned into a huge, free concert. Woodstock also became a massive logistical disaster: hundreds of thousands of people without adequate food, water, sanitation, shelter or other basic necessities. By the time we were done walking through the museum, we were impressed by the stories of cooperation, peace and goodwill that characterized the four days. Given our background, we were also impressed with how the emergency management was handled.

Although the governor of New York, Nelson Rockefeller, was considering calling in 10,000 National Guardsmen, the organizers convinced him it was unnecessary and could actually create hostility where there was none. The county did declare a state of emergency, and instead of the declaration resulting in crowd dispersal, curfews or other restrictions as it could have, local law enforcement and police reinforcements from the City of New York were actually more lenient. While there were some injuries and two deaths, they were accidental. One death was by drug overdose and the other the result of a tractor driver not observing a boy in a sleeping bag in his path. Violence wasn't an issue. The event had been billed as three days of peace and music and the huge crowd maintained that atmosphere throughout.

I got a kick out of watching the CBS News broadcast from August 18, 1969, on YouTube recently as iconic anchorman, Walter Cronkite, and two other reporters covered the Woodstock story. With Cronkite introducing him, John Lawrence of CBS News offered what sounds to our twenty-first Century ears like an amusingly dated analysis of the event[1]:

> "What happened at White Lake this last weekend may have been more than an uncontrolled outpouring of hip young people, struggling as they did to survive, first the twenty-mile traffic jams and five-mile hikes, then the intense heat and sudden rain, the thirst and hunger from the shortage of water and food, just for the opportunity to spend a few days in the country getting stoned on their drugs and grooving on the music.

> What happened at White Lake was that hundreds of thousands of kids invaded a rural resort area totally unprepared to accommodate them among adults who resent and reject their youthful style of life. And that somehow, by nature of old-fashioned kindness and caring, both groups came together in harmony and good humor and all of them learned from the experience.

> For adults who were there, it was a revelation in human understanding. They had not been aware,

---

[1] *CBS News with Walter Cronkite*, August 18, 1969. See https://www.youtube.com/watch?v=WehjMZcQqPA

as the kids are, of the gentle nature of young people to one another. These longhaired, mostly white kids in their blue jeans and sandals were no wide-eyed anarchists looking for trouble. Despite the overt appeals for violence by the few political radicals among the crowd, they remained polite, passive, and finally, as the area was saturated, helpless.

At that point, the residents of the area, learning of the emergency, began to respond. Housewives handed out hot coffee to stranded youngsters who had not eaten in days. Catholic nuns passed around sandwiches made by Jewish mothers. And the police, many of them from the violent precincts of New York City, invoked the law of practicality and allowed the kids the freedom to take their drugs in public. So many people were smoking pot, the police explained, there were not enough jails to hold them. A situation to remind the older generation of conditions 35 years ago, under which alcohol was legalized.

So that what was learned at White Lake was not that hundreds of thousands of people can paralyze an area and break the law but that in an emergency at least, people of all ages are capable of compassion. And while such a spectacle may never happen again, it has recorded the growing proportions of this youthful culture in the mind of adult America. Walter..."

And with that he passed the broadcast back to Walter Cronkite, who signed off with his classic closing statement, "And that's the way it is this Monday, August 18, 1969. This is Walter Cronkite, CBS News. Goodnight."

It was interesting to hear their choice of words regarding the crowds and their construction of meaning as they explained what happened. While it felt good to hear about the cross-generational cooperation that turned into a learning experience for all involved, I wonder, had the crowd been black instead of white, would the "outpouring" they spoke of have appeared as benign, and would they have been able to see the stories of "old fashioned kindness" throughout?

The way the political and law enforcement authorities observed, assessed and responded to the crisis of hundreds of thousands of peaceful "protesters" made it possible for Woodstock to become an iconic representation of peace and love or recreational drugs and rock and roll, depending on your perspective. Watching the old footage, it's easy to consider a hypothetical alternative to the historical narrative of Woodstock and the Summer of Love. Had the 10,000 National Guardsmen arrived on the scene to control or disperse the crowd, it's not likely there would still be concerts happening at Bethel Woods and we would have a very different national narrative about that event.

Just a year later, at Kent State, the authorities made different choices regarding the response to college students gathering to express their opinions, and the Ohio National Guard shot thirteen unarmed students, killing four and wounding nine. What would have happened to the individuals who attended Woodstock if they had been characterized as troublemakers and their presence and peaceful protest had been met with military force? Rather, their youth and their color were assessed as non-threatening and the response was largely compassionate and parental. Obviously, that wasn't the case with many peaceful gatherings in the 1960s and on through the years to the present day.

There's a lot we can learn from our past. It is possible for all of us, our elected officials especially, to work to understand and exercise authority from a position of greater insight, forethought and compassion, discerning the best course of action for the greatest good.

Hippies and
Hallelujahs

Our little family climbed out of our Volkswagen van and followed a group of hippies toward the bluff. Dad led the way, carrying Karla. He looked incongruent with the long-haired crowd, sporting his crew cut, horn-rimmed glasses and Bermuda shorts. Mom followed in her smart-looking summer dress and sandals, holding Karen's hand to make sure she didn't run off as she often did at that age. Linda and I trailed along behind in shorts, t-shirts and flip-flops. We all climbed over the rocks and down toward the beach at Pirates Cove, Corona del Mar, for the first time that summer of 1970.

Although we were early, a small crowd of people was already scattered over the usually quiet beach and hillside. We could catch occasional phrases drifting up from two guys in swim trunks sitting on a large rock, strumming guitars and singing. The crowds grew, and before long there were informal lines and clusters of teenagers and other young people waiting their turns to walk out into the water, moving toward two men who would talk briefly with each one before dunking them into the ocean in typical baptism style.

Once again I felt that childhood, swing-set rush of freedom and uplift of heart. Love, God, and joy were tangible out there in the ocean breeze. They were in the shimmering lambency of millions of light-refracted diamonds stretching as far as my eyes could see and reflected, too, in the faces of those walking back out of the surf, coming up drenched and happy.

My mother's childhood friends had a house on the sand in Newport Beach. Looking back, it was the quintessential ocean retreat of that era, with sand and woven grass mats on the floor, strings of shells hanging between doorways, rattan furniture, scattered plastic beach toys and abalone shells. We would spend the occasional weekend there or at rented summer shacks, playing with friends or sisters, digging holes in the sand and swimming.

Our church at home in Pasadena was large, structured and traditional. We had stained glass, organ music, robed choirs and four pastors, all men, who wore vestments and sat in big chairs on the platform for morning services. I had already been baptized earlier that year as part of my admission process to membership after attending classes and demonstrating I understood our church's theology. But, in spite of the traditional formality and visual evidence of authority, the leaders of our church encouraged us to pursue our own Bible scholarship. We were Congregationalists, and one of the central principles of our denomination was the equality in the priesthood of all believers.

Somehow, although my parents are still the most loyal, kindhearted followers of human authority one could hope to find on the job, in a church or in an organization; they are also antithetically and casually intent on following wherever they believe God's love and grace leads. This put our little family smack dab in the middle of what was called at the time, the Jesus People Movement.

Their intention to follow love and grace also explained why we had a constant stream of ethnically and nationally diverse visitors in our home in a time when our neighbors only grudgingly approved their presence. On more than one occasion, my mother made the rounds specifically to inform them not to mistakenly call the police when they saw our invited guests leaving our house at night.

It was only as I wrote these stories that I recalled that love and grace also explains why we would stop in front of the Sirhan home on the way to school during the fall of 1968, while one of us ran to the door to knock and pick up the mother of the man accused of killing Senator Robert Kennedy. Mary Sirhan, a Palestinian Christian and refugee who had suffered much in her life, had accepted the invitation of friendship offered by the circle of women Mom was a part of, and for a while she attended Bible study group. The off-the-cuff way my mom explained the various connections we experienced with people calibrated my heart to the belief that loving one's neighbors was something to be widely applied.

In that season of the late 1960s and early 1970s, when God's love seemed to live most convincingly down in rural Orange County, our folks would load up the VW van with snacks, picnic dinner, and pajamas so the little ones could fall asleep on the ride back home. Then we'd pile in and commute evenings and some weekends to either the little church in the middle of the bean fields near the ocean or a beach somewhere to spend time with the hippies who were in love with Jesus.

Sitting cross-legged on the floor at the front of that little church, my convictions were validated. I remember listening one night as one of the hippies taught from the love passage in 1 Corinthians 13, ocean breezes stirring the room since one wall of the building had been opened to accommodate the barefoot crowds that overflowed onto the patio. He shared a song he had just written to help us remember that if love wasn't flowing through us, our lives would be meaningless. That was a lesson that continued to repeat in my life: without love, any noble action or sacrificial effort would not produce lasting good. Love must be preeminent, authentic and real.

Revolutionary Love

The windows were open to cool our crowded living room where I sat cross-legged on the floor with my girlfriend Missy and our siblings. Above us, making a rough circle around the room on the sofa and an assortment of chairs, sat another fifteen to twenty adults, an even mix of Africans and Americans, men and women. One of our friends strummed a guitar and led us in singing a familiar favorite in Swahili, "Tukutendereza Yesu."

As we finished the song that night and the room became quiet, Festo Kivengere leaned forward from his place on the sofa where he was squeezed between his wife, Mera, and my dad. Festo and other Ugandan Anglican bishops had recently gone with Archbishop Janani Luwum to meet with president and tyrant, Idi Amin, about his soldiers' acts of cruelty and violence against the people of Uganda. Their hopeful and brave intentions, along with their best efforts, ended tragically.

In his British-influenced English, Festo began to describe the streets of Kampala, the people and different sights and sounds from that day he had waited outside

Amin's quarters with agitated Ugandan soldiers for Archbishop Junani Luwum to come out. Festo was a storyteller and had a way of making the distinctly African scenes from his capital city feel like something familiar. For instance, he had often found ways to connect his struggle to love and forgive Amin's cruel actions in his country to all of us and our need for love and forgiveness here. His words always felt relevant to my life in America. These kinds of stories from different African brothers and sisters, as we called one another, encouraged me in my own understanding of place and responsibility in the world.

A few weeks before, Festo had told us, with Mera filling in details, how Amin had taken their dear friend Luwum into custody while Festo and the other bishops had been allowed to return to their homes. They heard through witnesses that the Archbishop had been beaten, tortured and murdered. The formal government report to the public was that the Archbishop and two other ministers had been in a car accident. People who knew the truth about Luwum's death also knew of Amin's intent to kill Festo as well and had urged him and Mera to escape, persuading them that they could do more for Uganda alive than dead. After briefly struggling in their decision to leave the people and country they loved, Festo and Mera had driven through the dark countryside to the mountains and climbed over them through the night into Rwanda, where others had helped them continue their journey of escape.

As he sat on the sofa, talking about the recent events that had brought them to Pasadena, Festo choked with emotion at losing his friend and mentor. Emphasizing his feelings with his hands, he shared transparently from his heart. He frankly confessed the fear, anger and bitterness he had felt toward Amin, sharing the hatred he experienced as he realized that even the life of his loving and noble friend had meant nothing to the dictator.

Our African friends had a phrase, "walking in the light," to describe this kind of honest discourse or confession, where one's sins, failings, raw emotions, and even harm one has done to another is admitted publicly by the transgressor. We could be forthcoming and walk in the light because the light was the grace and lovingkindness of a forgiving, healing God. I remember a story Festo would tell about a little girl who asked her father what God did all day. The answer was, "He fixes broken things."

In humility of heart, Festo walked in the light that night with us, confessing the ways his response fell short of Christ's, who had been able to forgive the hypocritical religious authorities and the Roman soldiers who were torturing him to death. These Africans, who were connected to Desmond Tutu and others who led many conflict resolution movements on the African continent, believed the only way to move forward as democratic nations made up of citizens with equal rights and protections under the law, was to journey together toward forgiveness. They modeled for us how to walk in the light by bringing selfishness, sin and evil out of the shadows and into the light. Walking in the light was the first step in the long process of achieving restorative justice and necessary healing from egregious atrocities.

Festo also spoke that night in our living room about the ways in which God was putting an inexplicable love in his heart. He was continuing to grow in his belief in God's love for himself in spite of his struggles to forgive and he was discovering a growing love for the man, Idi Amin, where hatred for the dictator had been. He spoke of amazing grace that makes the impossible possible. He went on to write the book, *I Love Idi Amin.*

The love that all of us require has to eclipse adversity, tragedy and loss, and must be powerful enough that a person can even love one's enemies. Festo called this "revolutionary love."

Mobs and Bullies

Suddenly a crowd of fellow high school students came rushing toward where I was sitting on the stairs outside the gymnasium with my friend Lorraine. For no clear reason we could make out, another pack of kids came bursting into the grass corridor between the buildings, upset and yelling angrily.

Some in the stampede turned to chase others up the stairs. Everyone was pushing and jostling each other as they ran along. Here and there someone was knocked to the ground, accidentally elbowed or deliberately butted against the walls. Two guys, chasing a boy on the second-floor walkway, shoved him so hard he tumbled over the side. They kept on running as the boy managed to grab the edge of the railing. Thankfully, others coming behind helped him swing back over to safety. He hunched, grabbing his ribcage in pain as the crowd moved by.

The shouting, roiling mob of guys turned the corner without noticing us, running out of sight around the building and toward the adjacent park. We couldn't tell if the two men trailing behind the pack, wearing the red jackets of our campus security, were running along with or trying to catch the students. It was impossible to figure out what this whole lunch outburst had been about.

We heard rumors later that the mob incident was started by some gang members from Los Angeles who showed up on campus to settle a score. I don't know if that was true and don't even remember how it all turned out. Every day of my freshman year at Pasadena High School, where the decision to integrate had been enacted a few years before, seemed to present situations that made no sense to me. Inexplicable happenings, some of them violent, became the norm.

Up until ninth grade, I had attended Pasadena Christian School where everything I experienced was strictly predictable. My world at home was filled with a changing montage of caring and compassionate people from around the world. By and large, kindness, good manners and intelligence ruled the day everywhere I spent time. That was normal.

I was a nerd. I had known it for years and there are pictures to prove it, but I don't recall it mattering one way or the other until those first days of high school. Everything about my appearance was fair game, and I quote here. I was a "honky bitch" (both interesting new additions to my vocabulary), "blind" (I wore thick glasses), had "bad hair" (like straw, evidently), was "colorless" (a freak of nature), and wore "weird clothes." This last one I knew the bullies were right about. (Knee-highs and a particularly ugly orange plaid dress elicited that comment. I was grateful for the input. I never wore it again.)

I was told I didn't belong. As it turned out, I especially didn't belong in any restrooms. I learned this after being pushed against a wall and told by three black girls that this was their territory and not to come back unless I wanted to be f***ed. This was a problem. I solved it by not drinking any fluids on school days. I would wait until sixth-period gym class where I could use the bathroom in safety because my older volleyball teammates made it possible with a united show of strength.

My parents were not really engaged in the difficulties I faced at school. There was a lot going on with the four of us girls going different directions with sports, music and other activities. They didn't understand at the time how physically threatened I felt. I think they also simply believed in my ability to negotiate and see my way through trouble.

Being bullied in high school was painful, but ultimately I learned how to avoid the spaces on campus where it was most likely to happen. I sought out friends. Also, I had a convincing, gut-level understanding from childhood that the cruel comments were only aimed at what was skin deep and that none of those traits had to do with my worth as a person. I was able to make it at school.

My story isn't unique. School experiences can be rough on anyone. I know being bullied for what you look like resonates with many people of every ethnicity across the country, but perhaps it's most familiar to those of us who were part of efforts to desegregate the schools. The Pasadena School District was the first outside of the South to be federally mandated to integrate. For me, the turmoil around the issue of racial integration became personal. I attended private school during the years busing first came to town, so it wasn't until I began public high school in ninth grade that I discovered what it was like to be treated poorly simply because of the color of my skin.

In addition to the bullying, the education system got involved. At the end of ninth grade, I was told that the district needed more white students at the high school across town. No longer allowed to attend school in my neighborhood, I was bused to John Muir.

The need for integration began with the discrimination that has always been present and suffered by those in the minority. Until Brown versus the Board of Education in 1954, those inequities that pertained to color had been intentionally and willfully overlooked by white society. Busing students to achieve racial balance was a judicial response to our nation's long history of white, ethnocentric thinking that deliberately treated non-white as unequal in every arena of life. Historically, inequality most glaringly shows up in our nation's schools and with our children's educational opportunities.

When we were working in Arkansas after the ice storms of 2009, we got to spend time at the Little Rock Central High School National Historic Site Visitor Center. For me, it was healing. I was reminded again from the stories of the heroic Little Rock Nine, who were the first black students to attend an all-white high school in the South, that my integration stories from California are relatively benign. Mine are hard and impactful, but in comparison to their experiences, I had a walk in the park. Those students were warriors, and suffered not just at the hands of their peers, as some of us white kids did during busing but from the deliberate actions of adults and the local, state and national institutions their parents' tax dollars went to support.

But being harassed and bullied as children isn't exclusive to racially motivated conflict. Students have been pushed around for being different for centuries. People from other generations and countries have shared their stories with me of being hurt and tormented growing up in school, dormitory and team settings. Children and young people left on their own often create a culture of one-upmanship and domination. So do many who don't "put aside childish things" in order to really grow up.

Lord of the Flies, required high school reading in my day, illustrates the principle to the extreme. A group of English schoolboys, marooned by a plane crash on an island, create order and hierarchy amongst themselves, seeking to replicate the world they came from. Initially, it appears that the guidance of a few boys will lead to productive results for all the boys. But, the only concept of order they knew or understood was from the life they had known in England, where adults had modeled authoritarian power and control. Leadership was entirely dependent on power *over* instead of power *with*.

Some of the boys became aggressively competitive, built twisted relationships with one another and overall caused everyone to live in terror. Seeking to have power over others, they subverted any possibility of developing a loving brotherhood. Ultimately, the result was murder and mayhem. The island paradise that could have comfortably sustained them all had they worked cooperatively was instead destroyed by fire. It's difficult not to draw parallels to our increasingly contentious culture in the United States.

A society built on one-upmanship and competition never makes sense but especially in the context of crises and disasters. Yet in America, we tend to accept and accommodate competitive, self-serving attitudes and values, even cheering them on in the sports we love, the shows we watch and the markets we invest in. We often applaud that kind of leadership as long as they're making the decisions that suit our personal interests. If others are handling the responsibilities and challenges of living in a democratic republic, we don't want to have to think about it.

My understanding of our democracy is that we're meant to participate, exercise our power *with*, and function as one body like it says in our national motto, "Out of many, one." Of course, that reference was intended to describe the unity of the original colonies, but it's also descriptive of how individual citizens form a singular identity as resilient Americans, not by being the same but by being interdependent and complementary. Diversity can work powerfully to our benefit.

My faith tradition and the study of basic physiology taught me the same. In an analogy from 1 Corinthians 12, the human body is used to illustrate dynamic community life. Each person is a different part of anatomy. If one individual believes they're not connected to another because of their differences, it's like the foot saying to the hand, "Because I'm not like you, I'm not part of the body." It's blatantly obvious that a hand and foot can both be part of the same body. To think otherwise is silly. Body parts don't function by themselves or in groups of other matching body parts. Similarly, we human beings each need others to form a vigorous, well-designed whole. All the body parts together make for a functioning body.

During a disaster, we all watch for the stories that show us time and again how Americans possess great human compassion, willing to risk life and limb to save others. What we need is that larger, "we're all one body" perspective every day in our life as a society. That ideal makes it possible for all of us to win.

Muir High Bus

I followed my little sister onto the school bus one fall day in 1974, a few weeks into the first semester of my junior year. Looking to find a seat, we quickly pushed past the packed rows in front, not wanting to anger our short-tempered driver, who rightly insisted that students be seated when the bus was moving. As was usually the case, there weren't any empty benches for the two of us to sit together, and we each looked for a single with the least hostile-looking seatmates. My sister found a spot next to a girl who looked up with a lift of the chin and a shrug when Linda stopped by her bench. I moved on and sat down a few rows back with a girl who reluctantly pulled her backpack onto her lap to make room for me.

The bus pulled into traffic on Hill Avenue, headed back across town toward our high school campus. I heard some snickering around me and, trying not to attract unwanted attention, figured out that the source of amusement was a boy with a cigarette lighter. It took a moment to see it wasn't simply the lighter drawing attention. I thought maybe he was lighting a joint, an act that might explain the laughter and growing sense of agitation around me. Slowly the scene came into focus. A few strands of my sister's hair were hanging over the back of her seat and the boy was waving his lighter underneath. Stunned, I watched a piece of her hair singe and smoke.

I yelled and it's possible that others did, too, because he snapped his lighter closed and shoved it in his front pocket.

Linda remembers her tumbled emotions as she discovered what was happening and heard the attacker mumble, his voice close behind her, "I wanted to smell a white girl burn."

The bus erupted in noise. Students yelled forward, "This fool's using a lighter!" "Trying to catch the bitch's hair on fire!" "Girl's hair is smokin'!" "Boy, you're in trouble now!"

The bus driver looked up into her mirror, swearing, trying to drive and see what all the noise meant, "What's going on? Don't *tell* me I need to pull this bus over!"

The black girl next to Linda turned and yelled at the boy behind them, almost climbing over her seat, slapping at his head, "What're you thinking? Leave her alone!"

In a swift movement, my sister wrapped her hand around her light-blond hair at the nape of her neck, gathered it into a ponytail, and pulling the ends forward, she examined them for damage. Twisted backward in her seat now, facing her attacker, she looked at me through the yelling students, both fear and resolve not to cry in her eyes. She silently sent me the message that she was okay. I remember an overwhelming feeling of helplessness.

The driver signaled to pull over. The boy slouched in his seat, smirking as other students, whether approving or appalled, awarded him with attention. The bus pulled to the curb and the driver squeezed down the aisle, following fingers and incriminations, until she got to the boy, stuck out her hand, demanding the lighter and telling him to sit up front for the rest of the ride where she could keep an eye on him.

As far as Linda and I can recall, nothing more was said or done. No other adults got involved, and we went about our school business as usual that day after we reassured ourselves that only a small patch of her hair was singed.

In many ways, it was just another day in school. It wasn't the first time we experienced something like this, although this incident was one of the more dramatic moments. There were other injustices suffered in the gym, between classes and in the bathrooms. One day on the softball field, I watched from the infield as a young black man approached white, blond Colette, who was playing catcher and was standing near home plate alone, waiting for the next batter. He opened his coat to reveal a handgun. I watched, disbelieving, as Colette shook her head, shrugged and walked away from him. As he left through the gate to the nearby alley, I ran up to her and asked what had happened. She said, "He wanted money. I told him I didn't carry any in my gym clothes."

Those years were fraught with heightened racial awareness, born of a new necessity to understand our environment and other peoples' actions based on skin color and ethnic identity. There were a variety of events that emphasized race as the salient factor in different troubles. We overheard white bullies using despicable racial slurs, saw spontaneous fights between different ethnic groups erupt on the quad, and countless other racially motivated incidents. Certain students were mean and territorial based solely on ethnicity.

On the other hand, perhaps ironically, I mostly remember the fun we had. Our differences increased our sense of the ridiculous in our broader culture. We laughed and enjoyed each other a lot. Race wasn't a hidden issue that we were supposed to pretend wasn't affecting the way we all behaved toward one another. Many of us were trying to figure things out and find the words and actions that belong with racial and ethnic equality. There were times when a large portion of the student body worked together to make our voices heard in our city. I remember participating in a show of unity in front of the school, demonstrating that there was power for good in this integration experiment we were a part of. In a sense, I think many of us at Muir felt like we were sharing in a story about justice that was bigger than our individual school experience.

I think we didn't really process these events from our school days with many adults during those years because many of us at John Muir were learning together in the process of court-ordered integration. We were forming friendships and were able to see that the majority of students didn't feel animosity toward each other. Acts of violence based on race were mostly committed and encouraged by a few handfuls of bullies. In a tough situation, we were as likely to be helped by one color as another. Friendship wasn't exchanged based on race but on the basis of character.

But now that we're adults, Linda and I can look back and see that we were also getting on the bus, walking onto campus or going to football and basketball games in those high school years with a newly acquired sense of insecurity. We knew of other white kids targeted and beat up for no reason except their skin color. One friend, although he was tall and athletic, was vulnerable because of his light-blond hair and blue eyes. He was specifically singled out because of his appearance and severely beaten, requiring stitches and reconstructive dental work.

Linda and I realize we had developed an unconscious wariness that we didn't analyze until years later. We started noticing we were behaving differently with our kids than our parents had with us. We were more protective and wary. However, we also had the added benefit in those high school years of a larger perspective, coming from the home we did. We recognized on some level that the context of being targeted for our appearance might have been a form of retaliation based on decades of organized, systematic racism and discrimination against everyone who didn't look like us—white. Plus, I think we saw how students of all ethnicities suffered at times at the hands of those who were different from them. These situations made us more aware of the frequent and routine threat and the sense of danger experienced by many minorities.

The benefits of desegregation for me, and I think for many of my fellow students, far outweighed the very real difficulties. We built friendships that crossed ethnic divisions as we spent time together over the years. We got to experience the joys of diversity. Our potluck meals are probably the best example, as well as an apt metaphor. I have memories of a service club meeting where we each brought a favorite family dish. The table was spread with a wild feast of cultural flavors: fried chicken, greens, stir-fry, sushi rolls, noodles, tamales, lasagna, meatloaf, homemade bread and more.

Perhaps we could look at school integration as an opportunity for everyone to interact more—parents, teachers and students—strengthening the fabric of our country and by it, our resilience. Businesses and other organizations could sponsor fun programs to help the schools with extracurricular ways of bringing the community together. They don't have to be complex. Something as ordinary as sharing meals and food traditions together can build our sense of connection and strengthen the social infrastructure that already exists within our schools and education system.

What's in a Symbol?

"Ready! Salute!"

I looked down at my hands and up at the red, white, and blue flag hanging to the right of the chalkboard. Reassured that I knew which of the two was my right, I placed my hand over my heart and joined my teacher and kindergarten compatriots in reciting the Pledge of Allegiance. This solemn moment each day as my afternoon class began included the mysterious words about being an "invisible" nation under God. I thought that was pretty special. Our flag and our country had secret invisibility powers with God. This particular piece of theology extinguished itself unnoticed at some point before I humiliated myself by making it public.

I have several distinct childhood memories within the broader impressions of Old Glory flying over government buildings, schools, and on our front porch for particular holidays. All of these recollections represent and are a part of the hope I feel for the United States. This one from kindergarten is something I still mentally refer to because I continue to have a moment's hesitation when I'm instructed to do anything that involves "left" or "right." When my eye doctor tells me to look left, my hands twitch as I determine by feel which is the hand I learned to salute with and extrapolate from there. I know. Weird. These early memories are also stirred by the many opinions and emotions people express about right or wrong when it comes to flag and anthem etiquette.

Starting in first grade, when the morning bell rang, I joined our whole school in beginning each day together on the playground, facing the flagpole, standing at attention in rows by class, hands at our sides as a trumpet played *To The Colors*. A student holding the American flag folded in the traditional triangle would stand at the pole, and with help from another student, carefully clip and raise the flag, pulling on the cord hand over hand until it was flying at the top. A student on a staircase landing nearby that placed him on a level above our heads would shout, "Ready! Salute!" And the entire school of teachers and students would place right hands over hearts and recite the Pledge.

I had a sense of pride in my country as our voices sounded into the morning. I assumed we were all committing ourselves to the principles of unity, the need for higher wisdom, and seeing to it that *everyone* in our country and beyond our borders experienced liberty and justice for all.

In fourth grade, I was so stirred by the experience one morning that it occurred to me that it would be even better to be one of the kids who raised the flag or led the salute. I went and asked to be put on the list, only to discover I was disqualified. Girls were not allowed to raise the flag or lead the salute. I was stunned. It was the first time I was aware that I could be excluded from something simply because I wasn't a boy. It was also the first time I was played by the "separate but equal" argument. Ironically, it was my love of the flag and sense of patriotism that uncovered the fact that my liberty and justice as a girl would be limited by others' perceptions.

Going to the Rose Parade has been a family tradition since before I was born. The New Year's Day celebration was a reason for family to return home and was a joyful kick-off to a new calendar of possibilities. We would carry our lawn chairs down tree-lined streets, getting to the route early enough in the morning to guarantee great views of the school bands, fancy horses and Eagle Scouts carrying banners identifying the floats covered in flowers.

My first understanding of the sacrifices made by our military forces came when my dad, who was drafted at the end of the Korean War, suddenly got to his feet and stood at attention until the Marine color guard leading the parade marched by. Once a Marine, always a Marine. In the early 60s, it seemed the entire crowd stood with us. Our family still gets up en masse as the men and women in the military pass by carrying the flag to honor those among us who have served and sacrificed. In recent years it has seemed that many in the crowd remain seated, not understanding our gesture, although those same people will jump to their feet to cheer for their team bands playing in the game later that day. It makes me interested to know what the people around us are thinking.

In spring of 1976, my classmates at John Muir and I were enjoying our final semester of high school. Our graduation was reason enough to celebrate, but since July 4, 1976, also marked the United States' bicentennial, the year was even more exciting. American flags fluttered everywhere and red, white, and blue abounded in fashion choices, marketing campaigns and patriotically themed products. There was a sense of celebration that seemed to extend outside of our anticipation of graduating from high school and encompassed the entire country. For me, the American flag represented everything fun and grand about being seniors, 18 and American.

However, in April of that year, a disturbing incident took place in Boston that hit close to home for me and other students at Muir, and expanded my understanding of national symbolism. The event itself took away some of our blissful anticipation of ditch days, school graduation parties and bicentennial summer fun before college. I was reminded of it all recently, more than 40 years later, by a story I heard on the radio.

As with other iconic moments in American history, a photographer captured a spontaneous instance in time—like the kiss of the sailor and nurse celebrating the end of WWII in NYC—that illustrated something of the essence of the feelings in the nation. It was a picture that became representative of the school integration story taking place. For me, that picture felt deeply personal and connected to my own story. Pictures can sometimes cause us to see our human nature more thoroughly than words can and reveal deeper layers of a people, the way a metaphor or parable uncovers unrecognized truths.

White students in Boston had been angrily protesting federally mandated integration. Hearing about the protests, I was able to relate to what they were feeling. I knew what it was like to be "arbitrarily" forced to go to a different high school. It's deeply emotional and frustrating as a teenager to be disregarded as an individual and seen only as a puzzle piece in solving a system's statistical problem.

To the authorities in my school district as I finished freshman year, I wasn't a person who had just spent the last months navigating student chaos on a scary campus. No one helped me process what it felt like to be forced to leave the friends I made and the meaningful roles I had finally gained at a new school. I had only been a number, pushed out of my neighborhood where I could walk to school, and onto a bus across town to address the "white and black" issue. My skin had been needed to bring color balance.

So, my perspective of the Pulitzer Prize-winning image taken that day in 1976 outside City Hall in Boston contained an authentic ability to empathize with the white students who were protesting. I had every reason to identify with the protestors. Nevertheless, the picture shocked me and I found myself unable to understand the violent image. It was all the more searing because it had taken place in Boston, the historical birthplace of so many of the freedoms we supposedly embody as the people of the United States.

In the black-and-white photograph an angry, white, high school student, gripping a pole with a large American flag, lunges at a black man in a three-piece suit who seems to have his arms pinned behind him by another white student. Looking more like a spear than the symbol of our nation, the Stars and Stripes are being wielded like a weapon to bludgeon a black man. Ted Landsmark, the 29-year-old, Yale-educated lawyer on the receiving end of the younger man's anger, ended up with a broken nose from his unexpected encounter. As we passed the newspaper with the picture from Boston around the next day at school, struggling through our own misunderstandings, prejudices and stereotypes, we didn't miss the profound truths evident in this front page story during our nation's bicentennial year. Racism was still alive and well in the United States of America.

It wasn't that I inhabited a moral high ground that the students in Boston did not. But rather, I had been afforded countless opportunities by that time in my life to enjoy a diverse circle of love. I had a cloud of elders who had spoken and modeled the ways of forgiveness, reconciliation and fellowship. The harsh lines of the system's forced busing, as it intersected my life, had been softened, and were by that time drawing my boundaries in the pleasant places of belonging within a greater context of friendships, school identity and pride.

The picture of the flag being used as a weapon made a lasting impression on my heart. We Americans can't afford to simply dismiss or expunge our shadier characteristics. We can't simply pretend that shining the bright light of honor and glory on our flag and our identity as a nation doesn't also expose the darker historic things we have done and seem to conveniently want to forget. Forgotten history is in danger of being repeated. Like shadow puppetry, the negative images that become evident when light shines on a symbol may be exactly what we're called to pay attention to in that moment. We don't need to be afraid of our past and present injustices as a nation; we can be grateful they are exposed and address our history with intentional goodwill.

We are more beautiful, more colorful and more multi-dimensional than any object that's used to represent us. Ultimately, is it our flag that is precious or the people it symbolizes?

Fear Focus

The Africans would often tell us children what it was like growing up in their home countries, painting pictures in our minds of their childhoods, families and adventures. Although I may have lost some of the accuracy, I recall enough of a hunting story Festo told to get across the gist of it.

When Festo and the other boys in his village were too young to hunt with the men, they would work together to trap small game. In a clearing the boys would pound sticks upright into the dirt and lay a crude net over them, balancing branches and leaves on top. Then the boys would spread out, forming a large circle in the surrounding bush. Yelling and hitting sticks together gradually, they would close in toward the net, tightening the circle as they scared small animals and birds through the vegetation. As the creatures ran in fear from the noise, they knocked down the sticks, became entangled and ended up trapped under the net. Festo's point in telling the story was to never run in fear. Had the animals not been afraid of the racket, they could have run away, past the boys, escaping capture. The boys had no weapons, only noisemakers.

As Festo said, fear is a liar. Festo believed perfect love casts out fear. Fear and anxiety don't exist where love rules the day. Decisions made when we are concerned, anxious and afraid don't end well. Running from what we fear will not lead us to freedom, progress and innovation.

Fear doesn't motivate and sustain greater resilience. Over the years as Graeme and I have worked on different aspects of infrastructure recovery from a variety of disasters, we've seen how loss and failure become major influences in planning mitigation and shaping the next major disaster response and recovery efforts. It's very common to hear leadership speaking from their anxious concerns about the past, "We don't want this to go like Northridge... Katrina... Sandy..." or whatever the last, most difficult response and recovery has been. Yet if we structure today's plans only trying to avoid mistakes we have made in the past or what we think we foresee, we are fearfully retreating from imagined catastrophes. A fear-based perspective causes us to borrow negative experiences from our past to predict and populate our future, robbing us of our present opportunities.

Yet, remembering our history helps us to keep from repeating it. There is value in looking back with the cleared-eyed intention of seeing what went right and how that can be improved upon for greater success in the future. What is important is the essential role of strong, relational human communities and their intersection with the infrastructure systems that support them. The everyday rhythms and relationships within a community, the daily activities of individuals, families, neighbors, coworkers, and colleagues contribute most profoundly to ultimate, powerful resilience.

We can also learn from our mistakes. There is an obvious place for evaluating the errors made in the engineering, construction, organizational, sociological and political reasoning of prior events. It is important to assess what caused a natural hazard to become a human disaster since it may uncover the need for critical changes in systems, design, construction, laws, regulations and policies. We can use the experience and information gained from disaster to move toward our mutually determined goals.

The point is not to simply survive and recover from disaster but to focus on our society and its people, along with deliberate actions that build relationships and communities in positive ways that have secondary outcomes of prevention, mitigation, and synergistic recovery from all sorts of crises.

Change The World

The grey morning still had a bite to it as we began carrying items from the warm house to the truck. Our three sons and I moved quietly so as not to wake the neighbors, loading an ice chest, folding table, walkie-talkies, boom box, a jar of white paint, a small assortment of sheet metal and lumber, and cameras into the back of the truck and closed the tailgate. In March of 2006, efforts like this were fairly common, as all of us in the family pitched in, helping our two oldest sons with film projects for their classes at Chapman University. Braden, the youngest, was 14, and I was happy to have him at home with me while Graeme was deployed to Louisiana working on the aftermath of Hurricane Katrina.

Andrew and Ryan had an assignment to shoot a project on 16 mm film, and they sold their professor on allowing them to make a music video with the film stock. In collaboration with our friend Chris Falson, a singer-songwriter from Australia, they set out to make a music video for his song, *Change the World*. 8-year-old Kennedy contributed her acting skills, and her mom, Rhonda, was willing to drive her and hang out as long as it took. Miles, a buddy of Braden's and happy to pitch in as needed, was dropped off by his dad, Doug, just as we were backing out of the driveway.

A motley guerilla film crew in our loaded Toyota pickup and Dodge minivan, we drove toward the foothills and into Eaton Canyon where we'd all spent lots of time over the years hiking to the 35-foot waterfall and pool that John Muir described in 1918 in its more pristine condition as "the Yosemite of San Gabriel." As I set up the check-in table and "craft services" at the edge of the parking lot, the four guys carried the film equipment into the canyon to a spot they had scouted a couple weeks before among the tumbled boulders in the dry riverbed where a large, twisted sycamore grew out of the hardscrabble soil.

The guys had reached out to folks in our community to be extras, hoping to have a diverse patchwork of people to represent our world. Throughout the day, dear friends and family found me in the parking lot and then picked their way down among the rocks and boulders to take direction for their parts in the video.

It wasn't until I was down in the canyon, the guys filming me for extra footage, that I connected what we were all doing in Southern California with what Graeme was trying to do in Louisiana. Standing down in the dry arroyo, cut by past stormwater, it seemed almost as though I was actually standing where the flood surge of Katrina had scoured the landscape. The intensity of the images we had all seen of the muddy water inundating New Orleans filled my imagination. Into the barrenness of this spot on the outskirts of Los Angeles, a swirl of memories from the desolation of the communities in New Orleans, of water, homes and people awash in misery, seemed to flow past where I was standing as I sang along with the recording for the camera, "If we all love how we would like to be loved, we could change the world."

Since Graeme had left for the Joint Field Office in Baton Rouge months before, we would talk every night as he ended his day, him telling me the stories about the things he had seen and projects he was working on. The massive destructive power of nature and the devastation of so many people's lives, businesses, art and history churned in my mind's eye.

Many of us were still hearing the heartbreaking stories of loss from Hurricane Katrina. Although there were many positive, self-sacrificing, humanitarian efforts taking place, the details I heard from Graeme of the formal infrastructure recovery process continued to persuade me that we could do better as a nation.

Over and over that day our busy friends and family took time out from their packed schedules to show up and sing Chris' words, "If we all be who we are meant to be, we could be something special. If we all love how we would like to be loved, we could change the world."

Our friend Toni Gilyard, a gifted poet and an interpreter for the deaf at a local high school, came later in the day and signed the song as she sang. Toni's hands illustrated a world rotating to a new place—a revolution. I had a surging sense of hope as I watched her that we could learn as a nation to cultivate revolutionary love and do better, even in the face of devastating circumstances.

UN Golden Rule

As I paused in a hallway at the United Nations, people of many different ethnicities walking around me, a tour guide stopped and described how Norman Rockwell used a variety of local models from his small town in Massachusetts for his large mosaic hanging on the wall opposite me. I smiled when she pointed to the rabbi at the center and noted he had been sketched using a model who was actually a devout Catholic and the retired postmaster of Stockbridge. As well, the Middle Eastern faces were from Rockwell's neighborhood market: the manager, Abdalla, and others from the store just a block from his house.

While we were living in New York City, working on the Hurricane Sandy recovery during 2013 and 2014, I had the opportunity to spend some time in the United Nations building. I had been thinking about New York's multi-faceted recovery process from the storm. What federal financial investments and mitigation efforts would best prevent future disaster? I turned a corner in the hallway, heard the guide and saw the beautiful glass mosaic, *The Golden Rule*, depicting men, women, and children of different ethnicities and cultures. Written in glass tiles were the words, "Do Unto Others As You Would Have Them Do Unto You."

In that moment, I recognized again that while it's important as a nation to increase the resilience of our public infrastructure, the truth of resilience is that it is fundamentally human and relational. The symbolism in Rockwell's process as he created a piece of art to represent the world community and the importance of mutual caring makes the subject even more profound. He found subjects to represent the world from among his neighbors. In truth, not just in visual appearance, the diverse cultures of the world *are* present within our American identity. Our multi-cultural diversity is a part of the fabric that makes us exceptional: E Pluribus Unum—out of many, one. Not just about many states with their different characteristics and cultures but our people, too.

Most faiths hold the principle of The Golden Rule and describe it in their own way. Many of us naturally believe in treating others the same way we want to be treated. This thought of reciprocity seems simple, fair and just to most people. It's the basics of good behavior, the standard on a school playground and the mantra of many parents training their young children to get along and treat their siblings as they want to be treated. "Would you like someone hitting you in the back of the head? Then don't do it to your brother."

But even the basics of good behavior are something not all of us seem to agree on. It's naïve to believe that, in their hearts, everyone wants to follow the Golden Rule. It's precisely our true motives that are inscrutable and most hidden, even to ourselves. Yet, I hear people use this as a defense of other's bad behavior. "They meant well in their heart." Actually, I don't think we know that. Simply put, many people place a higher premium on values other than love and human kindness.

I remember having a conversation with my Uncle Stan when I was about 12. He had stopped by the house near dinnertime and had been invited to stay. I must have been on post-dinner dishwashing duty that night because the two of us were sitting alone on either side of the table in the quiet dining room while the clatter of dishes in the kitchen from my mom and sisters cooking and setting the kitchen table insulated our space from the normal household hubbub.

I felt glad for this unexpected moment of connection with my uncle. At this point, he had served his prison time, and although I still thought he was cool and I loved him, to my way of thinking, he was in serious need of getting his act together. My dad and granddad had helped him get back on his feet with a job and apartment, but I could feel a palpable, underlying concern that he wasn't seeing the error of his ways. He wasn't pitching in like one of the adults in the extended family, and we rarely saw him, even though his daughter was living with us.

After we talked for a while about what classes I liked, he offered that he never saw any point in school and never shared my interest. He told me how he was thinking he'd quit his job and move on somewhere else. Not realizing I was asking an overly personal question, and reasoning from my limited experience as a child up to that point, I asked him how he was planning on taking care of his family. I must have posed the question in a way that felt religious or overly cut and dried to him, because he answered with a laugh, "But what makes you think I want to be good? I don't want to be good, that's not nearly as fun as being free."

I felt shock and then an immediate sense of dismay and sadness for him and all of us. He didn't want to be good. Goodness is a fairly straightforward concept to any child raised in a culture with Christmas lyrics that include, "So be good for goodness sake!" He thought freedom from a job and avoiding the cooperation needed to be a part of home and family was real freedom. He couldn't see the attractive beauty of love.

In the years that followed, this man I loved and had known to be loving and playful ended up on the streets. I remember hearing about my grandfather going in search of him on Skid Row in downtown, and the quiet grief and frustration that my grandparents, dad and his sister suffered. My "adopted sister" Karla grew up never knowing him or any of the cherished aspects of her father I got to see before his choices buried his life and hid who he was from our sight. We all suffered because he believed that his life was his alone and he was entitled to do as he pleased.

About ten years later, Graeme and I visited him as he was dying in the veteran's hospital on the other side of L.A. I had heard from family that he was mostly unconscious and uninterested in visitors, medicated against the pain of a failing liver, kidneys and other organs. He had been past help when the family got the call that he was sick and he was asking to go to a hospital. I sat next to his bed, holding his hand and talking to him about God's love, telling him how much I loved him. He told me he loved me and squeezed my hand. It felt like an unexpected gift. He died a few days later. His beliefs about freedom and goodness had played the thief.

With our current technological and scientific ability to observe how interconnected every aspect of our rivers, oceans, land and climate are, how dependent our fragile water and food systems are, and how interdependent we all are within our nations as well as globally, it's surprising more of us aren't seeking to live the Golden Rule. It's easy to see how doing so would ultimately benefit every soul on earth. If we lived it and applied it broadly, not just to our particular "in group," we would each be better off and the life and world we experience now and leave for our children would be more whole, beautiful and functional.

In making the mosaic that hangs in the UN, the artist used countless small, multi-colored, glass tiles that emphasize Rockwell's work more thoroughly. Just as it takes volumes of multi-colored tiles to communicate the simple message of the Golden Rule, it takes a large variety of people to create the reality of a whole world. Loving others as you love yourself is powerful.

Rockwell's use of diverse local Americans to portray the people of the world is a beautiful picture of the cultural wealth we have when we recognize we are stronger together. Vital solutions to the problems we face, new inventions and innovative thinking may come from those very people who are currently disenfranchised or newcomers to our country. As hard as it is for some of us to believe, our growing diversity and population can be our greatest asset if we simply choose to embrace this powerful and shared ethic of the Golden Rule.

Tit for Tat

"Ram her back, Diane! Ram her back!" I looked up from the tumbled doll in my toy baby buggy to see my mom standing on the front porch, yelling her advice to me about how to handle my playmate's repeated bumper-car-style attacks. As the story goes, I appeared puzzled by my mom's instructions as I tried following them, giving my friend's buggy an unconvincing push with my own. We went back to playing, emotions diffused, not because I "rammed her back," but because of the break in rhythm and my friend's chance to cool down. No harm, no foul.

Mom, satisfied, stepped back into the living room where she had left the women in the Bible study group she'd recently joined. One of the women spoke with a humorous smile, "Jan, do you think that's what Jesus is telling Diane to do? Hit her back?" As cliché as that sounds now after decades of the hypothetical reasoning invited by What Would Jesus Do? bracelets, the practicality of the thought was a fresh perspective for Mom. She recognized for the first time how a relationship with God was intended to change her relationship with others.

In the 1940s, when my mom was a little girl, she and her sister would occasionally swim at the pool in Brookside Park in Pasadena's Arroyo. She enjoyed her play times there and recalls her troubled confusion when she heard from friends that people who weren't white were only allowed to swim there the day before the pool was to be drained and cleaned. Intuitively, she knew there was something wrong about this rule.

When I was a teenager, a Japanese American friend laughingly told me that as teenage boys her father and uncles had been among those excluded from swimming at Brookside. As their own act of defiance against the hateful rule, they would sneak in at night to pee in the pool. It's a natural and understandable reflex to want to get back at or hurt those who have grieved and hurt you. Boys peeing in a pool is certainly a less hostile act than government-sanctioned racism. Still, my perspective or lens was my mom's story, which included grief over her mother's death when she was a child, her joy in swimming, and knowing she had been personally distressed when she discovered not everyone could use the community pool. It made it harder for me to laugh with my friend. For reasons that felt tender and important to each of us, the same story stirred up different emotions.

The "us and them" thinking that caused the pain can't remedy it. We need something more powerful. The ache in our culture continues to be multiplied and perpetuated when we only act out of our hurt and frustration. For those who daily experience systematic injustice, the challenges are immense. Still, learning to both care for ourselves and equally for others will help us recognize the ways to move our culture in increasingly positive directions. We must seek to find those things that move hearts and attitudes toward valuing restoration and setting right what has been harmed.

How Many People Does it Take...

Andrew took the package of clothes just delivered to his desk at the studio and went to try them on. With a grin he jogged back into the Visual Effects (VFX) supervisors' office, spinning in a circle, arms raised like Rocky.

"Good news, guys! They fit!"

It was late in post-production and the date for the release of the summer feature necessitated the usual innovative thinking required to be successful in the consistently under-budgeted art of VFX. Our son Andrew was a VFX coordinator at the time and his team was working on *Premium Rush,* a movie about a New York bicycle messenger. There were still several shots needing more detail to seamlessly make the actor, Joseph Gordon-Levitt, look as though he was being hit by a car, flipping through the air and crashing to the pavement. The team needed to get pictures of the costume's texture as it moved, and Andrew was the right size to stand in as a body double for the actor.

That summer, Joseph gave an interview to Vanity Fair regarding *Premium Rush* that included a comment about special effects. Titled to attract as many readers as possible, *Joseph Gordon-Levitt Hates All You Actors Who Pretend You Do Your Own Stunts,* Joseph was actually trying to share his spotlight with others on the film team. In the interview, he was complimenting the four other athletes who did the bike stunts to bring his character, a risk-taking, crazily skilled cyclist, to life.

"Let's be clear: I didn't do my own stunts in this movie. I don't like it when actors say that they did their own stunts. I rode the bike all day, every day, but there's me and four other guys who all had different specialties on the bike... and they're all brilliant... And you know, the thrills in *Premium Rush* don't come from big CG sequences. They come from watching these really talented, skilled athletes do crazy things on two wheels."

As mothers are prone to do, I'd like to brag that a few of the thrills actually did come from the computer graphics (CG) my son and others contributed. The unsung heroes of most of today's visual storytelling, computer graphic artists, put in long hours, late nights and weekends working in post-production, creating effects and putting on the final polish.

In the same way the credits after a film just keep on rolling, listing more and more names of those who had a hand in creating the stories we love to watch, there are unseen numbers of people who are vital to our resilience as a nation. We would do well to see the truth that all the members of our society make up the picture of our corporate strength.

If someone in a mall notices a suspicious backpack left in a corner, or a janitor knows the most solid parts of a building during a hurricane, and they take action on behalf of others, they are helping us write a better, more resilient story. With a little thinking, most of us can see the variety of ways people such as baggage handlers, gas station attendants, truck drivers, sanitation workers, and many others are as important to our security and resilience as our heroic law enforcement officers, firefighters, military and other professional first responders.

Believing and valuing the many people contributing to our wellbeing as communities will be one of the outcomes of our collective change of heart. We will be a nation where children grow up wanting to contribute to the whole. Likewise, the positive attitude and compassion we bring to our work, our home and our communities can contribute to our resilience as a nation. When we as individuals care about others, whatever role we fill becomes important and meaningful. Ultimately, the jobs we do are less important than the people we are.

It's Personal

We were on FaceTime with our sons Ryan and Andrew, who live in Nashville. They were showing Graeme a construction problem they were working on with their kitchen remodel when he noticed a screen in the background with something about an earthquake. Ryan said they were watching an interesting documentary series about chefs and this one just happened to be about an earthquake in Italy. Graeme and I were interested, and after we hung up, turned it on. The opening episode of *"Chef's Table"* contains an anecdote about how a chef became a pivotal player in disaster recovery.

On May 20th and 29th, 2012, two significant earthquakes struck Italy. 27 people died and damages were calculated at about 12 billion euros. Buildings in the Emilia-Romagna area that had been constructed before stringent earthquake standards were implemented were most severely impacted. Additionally, as is often the case, businesses with buildings that were able to withstand the quake sustained devastating loss when equipment, material and product inside weren't prepared for severe shaking.

The region is known for Parmigiano-Reggiano cheese. Thousands of wheels of it toppled from shelves, threatening the cheese industry in the region almost beyond recovery. Massimo Bottura, the chef in the episode, found out through his local cheese suppliers that the cheese industry might not make it through the crisis. To help, Massimo did what chefs do and designed a recipe, risotto cacio e pepe, which required a large quantity of the locally made cheese and locally grown rice. Restaurants around the world put this newly created recipe on their menus, and purchases of the region's disaster-impacted cheese and rice dramatically increased.

Although it's not always apparent, the ability to recover from hardship is built into who we are and what we do daily. This chef was able to contribute to the recovery in a meaningful way because of the relationships he had with his vendors. The relationships of our collective daily lives and our care for one another are our greatest resources. The same characteristics of friendship and social connection that contribute to individual health, longevity and a high quality of living are also the most valuable assets we can have when responding to and recovering from a disaster. Positive connections with the people we live with and come in contact with during our normal routines not only help us live well and happily but also create the community resilience that is, of itself, a powerful component of preparedness.

The strength of the community before a disaster, or in other words, the relationships people have with family, neighbors, friends, colleagues and others, may ultimately best determine the strength and long-term resilience of our cities, states and nation. These interconnections and friendships make us more resilient than we would be on our own. In the simplest terms, what I don't know how to do, my neighbor may know how to accomplish. What my friend doesn't have, I may have in abundance.

True recovery occurs where we have strong relationships or connections with the people we encounter in our daily routines. We are far more interconnected and dependent upon one another for our wellbeing than we often perceive. It's not business, it's personal.

Disaster ABCs

Not long after we moved with our three sons back to Los Angeles to work on the Northridge Earthquake recovery, Graeme stood waiting at the door for our youngest son to come out of his preschool classroom. Braden, seeing his dad, got up from the table where he had been coloring with the other little ones. Wearing a black suit, white shirt and black tie from his stint as a ring bearer in my sister's wedding, he looked like a miniature Blues Brother. For the last few months, these were the clothes he wore whenever we allowed it. As he headed toward the door, his teacher raised his hand to his forehead in a salute, "G'bye, guv'nor!" Without missing a beat, Braden returned the salute and said, "That's Mr. President to you," and walked out the door.

When Braden was 4 he was convinced he was destined to be President of the United States. As his parents, we were naturally pleased with this show of determination in one so young. His passion for the presidency lasted until he happened to find out the president did not carry a gun or drive the cool, stretch limousine with the flags. Serving as president was no longer interesting. Braden had no aspiration to be the guy sitting in the back.

The fundamentals of disaster work in the United States are a bit like Braden's discovery about the presidency. It's not what you think. The following is a simplified, brief overview of the basics. Still, even these details may prove completely uninteresting, especially to those who enjoy the illusion that any disaster can be set right by superheroes, well-trained military personnel or the right team of expert professionals.

Many Americans form their opinions from television news and disaster movies and have unknowingly adopted inaccurate ideas of what to expect during and after a disaster in the U.S. Until March of 1994, when our inside view of the Northridge Earthquake recovery began, so had we. We're still learning.

One of the most misunderstood realities is that in the response phase it's highly unlikely that emergency experts will be able to rescue us the way we've learned to expect from daily life when our 911 calls produce timely police assistance, a fire truck, a medical team or an ambulance. We are dismayed when we watch the media coverage of the first phase of any major disaster and witness overwhelming problems met with severely inadequate responses. Public services are immediately stretched beyond capacity. Most people in a disaster and many viewing through the lens provided by media are surprised by this lack of immediate professional intervention. Yet practically speaking, this is the simple definition of disaster: everything stops functioning as normal.

The very nature of disaster predicts that our local first responders will be unable to save the day. Even more jarring, no one entity—whether first responders, FEMA, the National Guard or other military branches, mayors, governors or the president—will be able to swiftly and efficiently provide all the necessary search and rescue, medical care, building safety assessments, debris removal, restoration of power, water, roads, airports, and other services essential to daily life and public welfare. A large-scale, coordinated effort is required between a multitude of government, private and nonprofit entities, and the general public, to give critical assistance and restore functionality. And, if you're the one who is suffering and hoping for the help you need to survive and recover, all of this feels as though it takes an impossibly long time.

When we experience a major disaster, the more likely scenario is that each of us will find ourselves, our families, friends, colleagues and neighbors to be the only first responders on hand. Our personal resources and those of the people around us may be the only immediate provision we have for some time when emergency services are stretched past capacity.

At the onset of a large-scale disaster, Emergency Operations Centers (EOCs) are opened and staffed. The disaster is managed and coordinated by local emergency management staff, government agencies, key community and private sector entities, and often representatives from the local Voluntary Organizations Active in Disaster (VOAD). The EOC prioritizes the most fundamental community needs and begins to coordinate efforts in the region. Something important to keep in mind is that any disaster may directly impact the first responders as well. For instance, in an earthquake, a fire station may be destroyed, and roads damaged to the point of being impassable.

If an event outstrips local capacities, additional resources can be requested through and coordinated by the

State Operations Center (SOC). If that is not enough, the Governor can request (and may or may not receive) help from the federal government, asking the President to declare an Emergency or Major Disaster. FEMA becomes involved only after local and state officials determine the disaster is beyond their ability to respond.

Typically, during the initial response phase of a Major Disaster, the recovery phase begins by establishing a Joint Field Office (JFO). While EOCs)are often in permanent and well-planned facilities, the JFO is set up in whatever available space can be obtained quickly—an empty office building, warehouse space or a vacant department store. JFOs remain operational for months or even years; as long as the recovery continues.

We've found that many people believe FEMA automatically deploys at the first indication of disaster. Many folks also believe that FEMA becomes responsible for every aspect of disaster response and recovery. However, in reality, FEMA is not considered a first responder but rather helps manage and coordinate the response activities of other federal agencies with local and state partners.

What needs to be clearly understood is the federal government doesn't "fix everything" after a disaster. Over and over we've seen the dismaying realization hit people who have suffered the loss of their homes and businesses that recovering from a disaster at the individual and family level is only minimally supported by our federal, state and local governments. The reality of FEMA's system is that homeowner's, renter's, and business insurance is expected to pay for the bulk of individual recovery. The weight of our personal response and recovery rests squarely on our own shoulders.

FEMA's primary role and the majority of its finances are dedicated to the Public Assistance (PA) Program. PA funding is meant to restore the region's infrastructure. PA provides funds for response activities, as well as repair and rebuilding costs for things like highways, bridges, utilities, schools, hospitals and other facilities by giving money to state, local, territorial and tribal governments and certain private, nonprofit organizations that qualify for help under the Stafford Act.

Unlike in the movies, it's not unusual for recovery to move extremely slowly and the lives and livelihoods of the people who have been impacted by the disaster to be disrupted and stressed for months and often years until full restoration of homes, schools, businesses, normal police and fire services, utilities, transportation, hospitals, and more has been accomplished. Even the most prepared and equipped communities and the government structures and agencies that serve us aren't usually prepared for this type of lengthy timeline in disaster recovery.

The truth that always becomes evident during and after a disaster is that we all need one another. From our work in emergency management, we are convinced that it's the strength of our relationships that ultimately determine the nature and quality of real recovery. The strength of our routine, daily, social and cultural infrastructure is ultimately the foundation for the built public infrastructure we rely on day in and day out.

Preparing to
Survive—Together

Too early for a Saturday morning, we carpooled with our neighbor, Brian, to the local elementary school auditorium, arriving in "comfortable clothes and sturdy shoes" to get a half-day introduction to our city's Community Emergency Response Team (CERT. As we walked onto the playground where a couple of firetrucks were parked, we were glad to find coffee and donuts waiting for us, since we needed the caffeine and the boxes of sugar and sprinkles to help lighten the mood. As we put on our name tags, we talked with some of the several dozen other folks showing up to find out about disaster preparedness. A good turnout for a Saturday.

Brian, Graeme and I were hoping the hours ahead would have some fun in them to hold everyone's interest. Being prepared for disaster requires a serious mindset, but learning new skills doesn't have to. The four-hour introduction that day reminded us about basic Cardio Pulmonary Resuscitation (CPR), told us to locate our gas line shut-off valve for after an earthquake, had us practice lifting heavy objects off of mannequins using crowbars and lumber as levers, and gave us the chance to put out small fires with fire extinguishers. It was a start.

As I've mentioned, when an emergency becomes a disaster, many people are left without the basic help they need. What remains largely unseen and underreported is the powerful role played by average Americans. All of us—individual citizens, families, neighbors, colleagues, non-governmental organizations such as churches, food banks and hospitals, and diverse businesses such as trucking companies, grocery, hardware and lumber stores—are the ones who truly carry us through. If we the people of the United States know nothing else about a disaster event, we should know this: experiencing a disaster will almost certainly mean taking care of ourselves, our family and our neighbors for a period of time and relying on them to do the same for us. Our communal goodwill is our best plan for coming through disaster.

So, programs like the one we attended that Saturday are important. It takes about twenty hours of training to become a card-carrying member of CERT and wear the recognizable green vest and hardhat that identifies someone who's been trained and qualified to help in an emergency. Participating in CERT is a simple way to increase preparedness. Our friend Jeannie, a CERT Coordinator says, "Preparedness is like laundry. It's never done." CERT is a great way to prepare, in that you can actually check off a list until it's completed. Should disaster strike, you have the important skills and abilities to help yourself, your family and neighbors.

It would be great if everyone had CERT training, yet not all cities have invested in providing it. Even when a community offers CERT, it can be difficult for the average citizen to carve out enough time for classes. Many of us feel as though we're just surviving our daily lives. Our normal responsibilities alone can often feel too challenging to invest that much extra time and effort. Even so, finding a way to attend CERT or similar trainings will pay big dividends in peace of mind and preparedness, and is a great way to connect with people who also intend to be resilient in a crisis.

Map Your Neighborhood (MYN) is another community-oriented program for disaster preparedness, organized in a way that is conducive for strengthening neighborhood relationships. It's really as simple as meeting for coffee with your neighbors. Using MYN, neighbors gather to watch a video together, go through a short workbook, and share the information relevant to the neighborhood's preparedness. By completion, a neighborhood has a clear plan about what to do immediately after a crisis event and how to help each other until professional emergency personnel are available.

Years ago, we had the fun of volunteering for the first ShakeOut earthquake drill, started here in Southern California. ShakeOut.org now has participants from around the world, helping to create preparedness for many types of disasters by offering a variety of resources.

One of the things ShakeOut promotes is developing a simple reflex for staying safe in an earthquake: "drop, cover and hold on." "Drop" means to move to a posture of stability, close to the ground. "Cover" indicates covering one's head and neck with hands, or moving under a nearby sturdy piece of furniture. "Hold on" describes grabbing onto the furniture and moving with it as needed to stay covered.

Participating in any disaster preparedness program is an easy way to be better equipped to handle a crisis. Having instructors or curriculum guide you through materials can make the process simple. But if you don't have access to preparedness programs or your schedule is packed, the message, "You should be prepared for disaster!" can feel intimidating and defeating.

The good news is preparing for disaster can also happen in a series of small steps. Just buying an extra can or two of your family's favorite soup or chili each week and setting them aside on an "emergency" shelf in your home can be the start of a disaster supply and a simple preparedness routine. When you're dealing with your important family records, like immunizations, drivers licenses, or insurance policies, scan them and save them to a couple of thumb drives that could be stored in a different location such as work, with a trusted family member or friend, or in a safety deposit box. Make a "go bag" that contains a thumb drive along with some basic emergency supplies: water, food, first aid kit, walking shoes, solar blanket and other items. There are lots of resources available to get you started.

Perhaps the most important thing we can do is simply talk with family members, neighbors and friends before there's a crisis. This makes a great first step for improving the outcome in any disaster and the general quality of life. Positive social interactions increase resilience across the board. Discussing what kinds of events are most likely to occur in your area, deciding together what kinds of supplies would be helpful, finding out what you already have that would be useful in a disaster—like a ladder, saw, or crowbar—and knowing what folks are willing to share, can quickly increase a community's resilience. Every step taken to be more prepared is a significant one.

Nightmare on Poydras Street

In the months before Hurricane Katrina, I had a recurring nightmare that was so disturbing and vivid that it influenced the way I processed the news coverage as the disaster unfolded in New Orleans during those days in August and September.

In my dream I was in a large hallway in a stadium, urgently looking for a bathroom. Finding it, I pushed through the swinging "in" door with a sense of relief at having located the women's room, expecting to see the utilitarian line of sinks and gray toilet stalls waiting for me. Instead, every toilet overflowed with urine, feces and blood, covering the floors an inch or two deep and making the room unnavigable. A little girl was sitting in a sink at the far end, disheveled and crying. Most disturbing of all to me, in the dream, I turned away without helping her and went back into the hallway.

In the nightmare, a group of 12 to 18 men, Graeme among them, were walking by dressed in tan khakis and white polo shirts; each cradled a clipboard and looked to be doing official damage assessments. I assumed they were unaware of the condition of the bathroom. I tried to get their attention. I wanted them to recognize the importance of what I was saying but knew I wasn't being persuasive. I was feeling my own physical urgency and overpowering dismay over the little girl who needed help. It seemed in the dream that I had to have *their* help to help her. The men weren't interested in the condition of the bathroom, my dilemma, or the suffering child. They had more important things to attend to. I would wake up feeling angry and powerless.

At the time, like the typical Psychology major I am, I figured these bathroom nightmares held some personal meaning; perhaps they revealed my basic needs were going unmet or that I had turned my back on my inner child or that I felt unheard by the men in my life. Obviously, Graeme had reason not to like the script of this nightmare. He objected to his role as part of a group of uncaring men, in charge but out of touch with essential realities.

Up until this time, Graeme had worked on the state side of disaster recovery and our newly formed company's work had been for organizations in Southern California. When Katrina hit, we had just returned from vacation with friends on a farm in Northern California and, without a television, were only somewhat aware of the storm. In the days that followed and the response phase dragged on, we heard about conditions in the Superdome. Both Graeme and I wondered if those repeated bathroom nightmares had been prophetic. Basic needs were going unmet and reports were that those in authority were not keyed in to necessary realities.

Like many Americans, we wanted to be of help. We had heard that engineers were needed for the massive recovery effort. Eventually, our company was hired by one of the prime federal contractors. Graeme flew to Louisiana November 3, 2005, to begin work at the Joint Field Office in Baton Rouge, ready to do whatever was needed. He began work as one of the hundreds, sitting at desks in a former department store, sifting through the damage survey reports.

One of Graeme's first assignments was determining how to handle the massive damage done to cemeteries. He had to determine how numerous human remains, coffins, crypts and funerary debris that had floated away from cemeteries to wherever the water carried them—people's yards, store parking lots, the side of the road—were to be removed, identified (some of them hundreds of years old) and returned or respectfully arranged for in some other way. If the funerary material could be identified, what business, government or agency was responsible for it? If there were next of kin, how would they be found? Might descendants want a memorial returned to its original geography? Who would be responsible for that? Who would transport it? Who would pay the costs?

Disaster by definition includes all the unforeseen components that outstrip the capacity of individuals, the community and society to cope using their normal resources. There are *always* unforeseen components.

Although the National Hurricane Center and National Weather Service both predicted much of the devastation that happened in New Orleans and warned that levees could be overtopped or might not hold, the Superdome within those levees was used to house people who couldn't or wouldn't evacuate. The bathroom conditions of my nightmare became a reality as plumbing inside the "shelter of last resort" failed. The nation witnessed the larger nightmare of how natural hazards combined with human infrastructure and decision-making fails to provide the care we all want to see.

Once Katrina's response phase transitioned to recovery, the cemeteries were only one tiny corner of a disaster that exceeded straightforward assessment. Without clear, comprehensive and inclusive ideas for our desired end results, recovery plans are shaped only by the immediate problems that need to be addressed, the essential infrastructure that needs to be patched back together, and often, opportunists who see a way to profit or promote their own agendas.

As a democratic republic, we must recognize our own culpability when our systems and government structures fail us. We need to take the time to form opinions about our desired outcomes before disaster impacts our lives. Then we need to discuss those expectations at the local level, seeing to it that what we decide together is passed on to our regional, state and national representatives for them to enact on our behalf.

Natural Hazards
and The
Unthinkable

Hurricane Katrina, more than any other disaster before or since, revealed our need for a change of heart. We were all witnesses to the apparent disparity in the treatment of the poor, who were mainly minorities. As the result of time spent working on that recovery in Louisiana, we realized how much we didn't know and still needed to learn.

The University of Colorado, Boulder, houses the Natural Hazards Center that hosts the Annual Natural Hazards Research and Applications Workshop. Disaster research began as an academic discipline in the 1960s. Since then, wherever disasters take place in the world, a wide variety of researchers from different universities show up. They go to the field to gather whatever data is relevant to their research. Some seek to understand the science of natural hazards and impacts on the environment; others to assess infrastructure; still others are looking to discover psychological motivations or to observe sociological ramifications.

What we found the summer after Katrina during our first visit to the Workshop was a surprisingly collegial and cooperative atmosphere where academics from a variety of disciplines sought to move research findings into practice. There were also a wide variety of representatives from agencies and organizations, as well as other individuals like us, who came to share their experiences in the field. Surprisingly, we had fun and felt a sense of catharsis and relief in being in the company of so many people who "get it." We especially liked the meals we shared as we gathered and simply made friends, building the relationships that increase understanding and facilitate shared wisdom. We discovered that at the heart of disaster research science, and this particular professional gathering, was a legacy of friendships and mentoring.

One of those who was mentored during the early days of this field, and was known for doing the same for others, was Bill Anderson. Many in disaster research were the product of both Bill's, and his wife, Norma's, personal and professional attention. Among those is the current Director of the Natural Hazards Center and Workshop, Lori Peek. And, since we've learned so much from Lori over the years, we recognize we're a part of Bill's legacy as well.

At the Workshop barbecue in 2017, we talked with Norma about the reasons she founded the Bill Anderson Fund, which helps minority disaster research students already enrolled in graduate school by supporting them financially, connecting them to mentors in the field, and assisting with placement after graduation and beyond.

Norma described how Bill had always wanted to reach back and help bring along those behind him. Bill's untimely death in a bicycle accident in 2013 had come as a shock, and Norma felt there was unfinished business.

One of the disappointments Bill experienced was how few young people from underrepresented communities became a part of the disaster research field. He would often come home from all kinds of important meetings and conferences and throw up his fingers to Norma to indicate how many other minorities had been present, including himself. Often it was only one or two.

Bill's and others' research has studied the experiences of African American and other minorities, women and children in disaster. He was convinced we would all benefit if these stakeholders were equally represented in the profession. Our experience working on disaster recovery bears this out as well, as it is often minorities who suffer most extensively and have the most difficulty fully recovering.

Academic findings are relevant and can offer the opportunity for innovation and significant advancement for our communities' resilience where that research is valued, discussed, assimilated and implemented. There are storehouses of extensive and thoughtful studies regarding the intersection of people, natural hazards and disaster, ready to be utilized. There are researchers and academics wanting to contribute the knowledge and wisdom they've gained that will reduce risk, increase resilience and save lives. It's time our government agencies, businesses and other organizations take hold of and implement this valuable resource.

Another year at the Workshop barbecue, I got the chance to hang out for a while with Amanda Ripley, a writer for *Time* and one of the speakers that year. Our conversation progressed from topics about natural hazards and disasters to discussions about things like current movies, our travels, families, life lessons learned over the years and hopes for the future. I remember telling stories about being kids, things we learned in school and things we thought mattered in life. We both wrapped up saying it would be great if somehow all this insight and wisdom we were surrounded by could really make a change and set us all on a better path.

Amanda had recently published a book, *The Unthinkable: Who Survives When Disaster Strikes—and Why*. It's an intriguing and easy read. It's also surprisingly empowering, with a historical overview of disaster, disaster research, stories from survivors, and science about how our brains respond under duress. What I liked about it was how human and relatable it felt. Listening to Amanda's talks at the Workshop had inspired Graeme and me to quickly read her book. Hanging out at the barbecue and sharing our desires to make a difference motivated us to take the content to heart. For instance, Graeme and I fly differently because of Amanda's book than the unprepared way we used to travel. We've increased our likelihood of being survivors with some simple changes. We both wear closed-toe shoes on planes that would provide more protection than sandals or flip-flops that might come off in a crisis. We pay close attention to the safety talk we've previously ignored, now knowing that just by listening and looking at the pictures on the safety card we are improving our statistical chances of survival. And we make sure the shades in our row are open for takeoff and landing so that emergency crews would be able to see into the cabin.

Amanda's book covers even more interesting infor-mation. She describes a variety of research findings that explain things like why people delay making decisions in crisis, the way many people did in the twin towers on 9/11; why women were almost twice as likely as men to be injured evacuating; how the seemingly inexplicable risks people are willing to take by not evacuating during a hurricane may have more to do with their beliefs than their income or resources; and yet how money is the most significant contributor to death tolls during disasters.

Graeme and I got home from the Workshop that year and ordered dozens of *The Unthinkable* to give as Christmas gifts. Our friends and colleagues who read the book passed it on. Later, a university we had helped recover from a fire that had destroyed offices, classrooms, laboratories, and student and faculty housing invited Amanda to speak as part of their process of healing and learning from all they had experienced together.

Research from the field of natural hazards and disaster is essential to our growth and development as a nation. We must recognize the importance of being better informed about the challenges we face and the ways we can improve practice in America. The academic research available to us needs to be implemented in the way we prepare, respond, recover and mitigate disaster. If presented in engaging ways, research can be easily integrated into our daily lives, moving us beyond survival into greater understanding and resilience.

Supplies and Good Intentions

The semi-truck full of baby formula drove through the night to get the much-needed supplies to the families struggling to survive in the wake of Hurricane Katrina. As the day dawned and the scope of the chaos and destruction became apparent, the driver realized he didn't have a specific destination or strategy for getting his load to the people he wanted to help. Uncertain if he could make it back to the last gas station he had passed, he decided to lighten his load, unhitching the trailer and leaving it on the side of the road before turning around and heading back the way he came.

When we were doing research on a donation management project, we learned in a series of conversations with Larry Herman of the Midwest Food Bank about scenarios like the one above. Following Katrina there was an outpouring of charitable giving, as is the case following every disaster. Americans are generous. Larry described how the food bank, in addition to continuing to care for local needs, had also provided food and supplies to impacted areas in Louisiana and Mississippi, responding to specific requests from the

Salvation Army. In the course of delivering semi-truck trailers full of requested materials to designated emergency facilities in those states, Larry and his team discovered huge quantities of unusable donated goods were adding to the chaos and disorganization.

Uncoordinated "gifts in kind" are a very real challenge after disasters. These donations can be unusable for various reasons: trailer loads with too much of one item and without a strategy for distribution; old, unsorted clothing; products that are inappropriate because of timing, like laundry detergent for people without water; and products that are spoiled and have passed their expiration dates. In short, these materials create more problems than they solve, and interfere with the critical distribution of necessary supplies.

Larry and the team from Midwest Food Bank recognized the need and offered to transport the unusable donated goods back to their warehouse facilities, where the materials were sorted and strategically repackaged for distribution at the appropriate time and in the appropriate quantities, ready to be used. Using this strategy, many truckloads of unusable goods were turned around but not without a significant cost and loss of efficiency. This story represents only one of the additional crises that are triggered by people who don't understand disaster.

On January 12th, 2010, Haiti was struck with a 7.0 earthquake, and again we watched scenes of devastation and human suffering on television with a desire to help. It wasn't until May 2010 that Rich Stem, a colleague and friend made during the Arkansas ice storm of 2009, contacted Graeme about a transitional housing project being planned by the Salvation Army World Service Office

(SAWSO) for Jacmel, Haiti. Graeme arrived June 10th to begin work as an operations chief, going out each day with a translator, construction supervisors and crews of local trainees. By mid-July the project had accomplished all the government of Haiti would permit at the time, having completed 600 temporary homes, a significant effort for that city.

An interesting component of SAWSO's project was the origin of the lumber used in construction. Due to drought conditions, the western United States' forests had been suffering from an infestation of bark beetle, resulting in a substantial number of trees dying. A connection was made, allowing the damaged trees to be turned into strong and usable lumber for temporary transitional housing. One country's loss provided a solution for another country's devastation.

Since the Salvation Army has been building relationships in Haiti with community members and leaders since 1950, it's not surprising that their housing project moved ahead in ways others' efforts did not. The Salvation Army team recognized the need to work *with* communities to determine the most critical needs based on long-term relationships, rather than simply specifying what would be done for them. Once home sites were identified, the building process was streamlined by repackaging bulk materials (lumber, concrete, hardware, etc.) into housing kits that could be delivered efficiently. On site, locals worked on construction with help from outside expertise like Graeme's, augmenting their understanding of the process for the temporary housing project while strengthening their construction and job skills.

This kind of thinking isn't always present after disaster. As mentioned, during the response to Katrina, supplies were being sent to areas in need without a coordinated distribution plan in place and items meant to be of help became the cause of traffic and congestion where first responders were still needed. The same was true of unsolicited volunteers. There were stories of people showing up to help and needing their own assistance, unaware that they would require all their own survival supplies, including days' worth of water, food and gasoline for their return trip. Intending to do good, they became another liability.

There's a need to better coordinate disaster efforts with those who are in the community or who have relational roots there. There are many ways this can be improved. One idea could be the creation of intermediary teams of people with experiential wisdom that would interface between assistance organizations and the local governments' impacted leadership, other government entities, businesses and communities.

There continues to be a clear need for growing the nationwide standard and predictable consistency for the coordination of voluntary organizations. In part, that's why the National Voluntary Organizations Active in Disaster exists, to connect organizations to each other and offer them a unified point of communication between their organizations and government agencies working on disaster response and recovery.

There is also a need for an independent clearinghouse that helps place individual volunteers, from carpenters to doctors, chefs to architects—anyone desiring to help after a disaster. Individuals and families, particularly from poor and minority communities, have the most difficulty fully recovering from the hits sustained in disaster. With a clearinghouse, it is possible that not just volunteer organizations but also American businesses, individuals, and nonprofit organizations might participate so that more of our recovery efforts are seen to completion.

Disasters and Hospitals

My sisters and I thought Mom was shaking us awake in the dark one early school morning in February 1971. The whole house was creaking and everything in it was making a crazy, freight-train sort of noise. We heard Mom calling to us as she ran from her room, "Earthquake! Get to the hallway!" Jumping out of bed, we ran to the central hallway as the floor pitched. The shaking only lasted 12 seconds and had probably stopped by the time we were together with Mom, Dad and the four of us girls sitting on the floor in the dark, legs curled up. Even though it was over, our hearts were pounding in our ears and we had enough adrenaline in our systems to run a four-minute mile. As we talked and laughed in relief that the house seemed to be standing strong, we compared the experience to an "E-ticket ride" at Disneyland—code in those days for something exciting.

Until safety inspections could be done on the schools, classes were canceled. I was glad to get out of a math test. We spent the rest of that day close to home, feeling the decreasing aftershocks, listening to the radio and watching KNBC, trying to figure out what was happening in the rest of Southern California.

Our happy sense of an unexpected holiday diminished as we began hearing reports of how many homes were damaged and the number of people who were hurt. As aftershocks continued to rattle our house, we learned that two hospitals in San Fernando Valley, one of them newly built, had collapsed with people inside. Our family began to recognize the heartbreaking losses others were experiencing, and feel a sobering sense of gratitude that all of us were safe. The casualty list and death toll climbed over the next days as news coverage increased and bodies were pulled from the rubble.

I was 12, and the thought that people who had gone to a hospital to get well had been killed seemed especially tragic to me. Doctors and nurses who would have been helping people with earthquake injuries in the community had been crushed along with their patients. Those hospital images and the lessons about the critical role they play in a community's resilience have become repeated themes in our work as we've had an inside, albeit blurry, view of the politics of disaster funding.

As is so often the case in the United States, the tragedies that happened in the 1971 earthquake led to changes to improve building codes and strengthen our infrastructure. One upgrade came in the form of the Alquist-Priolo Act, legislation intended to prevent buildings for human occupancy from being constructed on or across the surface trace of known earthquake faults. Another improvement happened after the 1989 Loma Prieta Earthquake in the San Francisco Bay Area through the Seismic Hazard

Mapping Act, requiring the state geologist to identify and map additional areas of earthquake hazards.

After the Northridge Earthquake, as the result of the complex and complicated requirements placed on earthquake-damaged hospitals by the California Office of Statewide Health Planning and Development, FEMA developed the Seismic Hazard Mitigation Program for Hospitals (SHMPH). SHMPH (pronounced "shemf") used a fairly simple algorithm to determine funding amounts for structurally damaged hospitals.

SHMPH funds were required to be used to either: 1) upgrade damaged acute-care hospitals to allow for immediate occupancy after a seismic event or, 2) construct a new acute-care hospital to current building codes. Under SHMPH, FEMA awarded approximately $2 billion to Los Angeles-area hospitals.

In 2005, more than ten years after the Northridge Earthquake and just before Hurricane Katrina, our company was hired to help one of those hospitals hold on to the money they had received. FEMA was planning to take the funds back because the hospital had missed deadlines due to a series of unforeseen obstacles. The earthquake had compromised many hospitals, but this one had several additional challenges. Their facility was built in 1927 and was a registered historic landmark. Their building couldn't be upgraded to current codes due to physical constraints, and its landmark status further complicated possible repairs. Additionally, the geography of the hospital property didn't easily allow for construction of a new hospital building, and the administrators had been unable to find a suitable location elsewhere.

The amount in question was approximately $8 million and would have been a substantial help in moving the acute-care facility toward complete recovery after the losses sustained in the earthquake. Based on the spirit and intent of FEMA's Public Assistance Program, the hospital had good grounds to appeal FEMA's decision. Unfortunately, after much effort at the hospital's expense and a lack of support from their political representatives, the appeals were denied and they lost their funding.

As seems obvious, hospitals are a crucial and pivotal part of a city's resilience under any circumstance. Losing the opportunity to sustain critically needed acute-care capacity in the Los Angeles area, already substantially underserved, seriously compromises the community's overall resilience. It's important for all of us to recognize this, make sure our voices are heard and insist our leaders and representatives do what's best for the entire community.

When Hurricane Katrina slammed through New Orleans in August 2005, remarkably, Charity Hospital survived with minimal damage. The hospital experienced critical challenges but without the devastating loss experienced by other structures throughout New Orleans. In the aftermath of the storm, when the levee system failed, the basement of Charity flooded, along with the surrounding neighborhood, knocking out power and water systems and leaving the hospital isolated from outside resources and help. Like an island in the middle of the city, no one could come or go. Appallingly, the staff was stranded with several hundred seriously ill patients that they had been unable to evacuate. For nearly a week, everyone who was not in critical condition in the hospital worked under harsh conditions to sustain life and supply healthcare.

The patients and staff were finally evacuated by airboats that came, not because of a local, state or federal government evacuation plan but through the relationship a nurse's father had with someone who in turn had a connection to an official in the state's Wildlife and Fisheries Department.

In the next days, after patients and staff had left, various expert military personnel were brought in to clean, decontaminate and prepare the hospital to receive patients. Amazingly, Charity was functional again and in better condition than before Katrina within just three weeks of the hurricane.

However, inexplicably, the state chose not to reopen the hospital in spite of the facility's ability to provide critically needed care for the people of New Orleans who were more in need of it than at any time in their history. Over the following months of the recovery phase, FEMA teams assessed the damage to Charity Hospital at approximately $26 million. The state rejected that estimate and claimed it was entitled to the full replacement cost of the entire hospital.

As the state and FEMA argued over the extent of damages and repair costs, Charity Hospital continued to decay due to vandalism and neglect as minimal, temporary hospital services for the people of New Orleans were set up first in a parking lot, then the convention center, and eventually in a vacant department store. Ultimately, after Congress passed the Post-Katrina Act, a three-judge arbitration panel directed FEMA to pay approximately $475 million to the state to replace the iconic Charity Hospital.

The important priority of patient care was set aside to promote the plan Louisiana had developed, long before

Katrina hit, to close down Charity and build a new, state-of-the-art facility. Unfortunately, the plan to relocate and build a new hospital also included the destruction of roughly 70 acres of recovered and thriving New Orleans' neighborhoods through eminent domain. After the devastating losses of Katrina, the community also lost a nearly 300-year-old cultural anchor and decades' worth of solid neighborhood social infrastructure. The well-researched documentary, *Big Charity,* tells the story with expert testimonies and persuasive images.

Although Graeme was in Louisiana working on different issues relating to Hurricane Katrina recovery efforts and not working directly on Charity Hospital, we had a growing uneasiness as we saw the disconnect between decisions being made and the community needs of the people of Louisiana. It appeared that the priorities of the few with influence outweighed the best interests of the many.

In October of 2012, Super Storm Sandy swamped parts of New York City. In its wake, many buildings, subways and utilities in the city were flooded, leaving them uninhabitable and unusable. Included in the damage were several hospitals.

We moved to New York in April 2013 to help with the recovery efforts. A large federal contractor giving support to FEMA hired our company, and Graeme became part of the team that worked on several impacted hospitals over the course of the next twelve months.

During that time, the team spent thousands of hours quantifying damages, reviewing losses, and determining estimates of recovery costs in accordance with the Public Assistance Program and the changes introduced by the

Sandy Recovery Act. The final estimate was based on information provided by the hospitals and was considered a liberal assessment of the cost necessary to restore the facilities to their pre-storm function and condition. By the time we demobilized for a break back home in late March 2014, the team had developed an estimate of roughly $600 million for the repairs on one particular hospital.

A few months after we returned home, a colleague sent us a message asking if we had seen a New York Times article about the project. When we read it, we discovered that, based on the involvement of one U.S. Senator, the majority of our team's previous year's efforts had been ignored, and for no substantiated reason that we know of, FEMA had awarded the hospital over $1.1 billion, a $500 million increase.

It was hard for us not to be disheartened by the complete disregard of the work we and the team had done for over a year. When other hospitals in New York discovered that one hospital had been singled out for a windfall, they insisted on equal treatment and another $1.6 billion was given to four other New York City hospitals.

This information is all public and well known. You can Google it. Over the years we have been aware of many similar incidents where federal money moves at the discretion of different political players instead of according to FEMA's funding structures. In cases like these, the Office of the Inspector General in the Department of Homeland Security will often conduct costly and time-consuming audits to determine if funding has adhered to the laws, regulations and policies. Yet, even when funding has been taken away in an attempt to set things right, the amount of money wasted is extreme.

This lack of financial integrity is not confined to our medical lifelines. This type of problem is true with every other lifeline in the nation that pertains to community resilience as well. The decisions being made regarding the control of large amounts of disaster recovery funding and the strength of our infrastructure are tangled and intertwined with political and corporate interests. There is post-disaster funding being granted based on something other than the consistent application of the laws, regulations and policies that could improve national resilience.

Frequently it is not the public's best interest that is the driving force behind disaster recovery funding. This isn't simply a disaster recovery problem—the compromised and embattled state of our lifeline systems and the nature of government funding are simply seen more clearly when we look through the window of disaster response and recovery.

The current situation, where only a select few are ultimately responsible for the final decision-making on billions of dollars' worth of funding, doesn't serve our communities and our resilience. These individuals are able to undermine the efforts of those like us, who are trying to fairly apply the relevant laws, regulations and policies involved in disaster recovery. What is needed is consensus building and clear-eyed integrity unmarred by localized self-interest. We need leaders across the country who can work together because they genuinely care about the people whose lives, businesses and infrastructure have been devastated by disaster regardless of whose district they're in. As a nation, we need to do what it takes to see that all our citizens recover from disaster and we're *all* stronger for it.

Mexico to the Rescue

My friend Silvia, whose parents emigrated from Mexico, shared a Washington Post article on Facebook some time ago about Hurricane Katrina. She was dismayed because many prominent Americans had been expressing their prejudice and hostility about our relationship with our national neighbor to the South. Silvia wanted her friends to be reminded of a bigger picture.

The article, *When Mexicans Crossed Our Border to Feed Americans in Need*,[2] relates how the Mexican military became involved during Hurricane Katrina, speeding to the rescue to help, not waiting for an American invitation or approval before deploying necessary aid. By the time they were done in Texas, the soldiers served meals, distributed tons of supplies and provided medical assistance. In addition to the soldiers' work there, Mexican sailors arrived in Mississippi to clear debris.

---

[2] *Washington Post*, Stephen R. Kelly, August 28, 2015. See https://www.washingtonpost.com/opinions/when-mexicans-crossed-our-border-to-feed-our-hungry/2015/08/28/347342e4-4cee-11e5-84df-923b3ef1a64b_story.html?

Enjoying coffee together in a favorite bookstore, I brought up the article and Silvia described her heartache at the way the Mexican people, and Americans of Mexican descent, unfairly suffer the brunt of uninformed and sweeping bad opinion. She described how personal and hurtful this feels. To illustrate, she related a story. Recently, she had been out at a Mexican restaurant with friends when they noticed a young man at another table wearing a t-shirt with a derogatory comment involving prostitutes and her childhood hometown just across the Texas-Mexico border.

One of her friends at the table said, "Well, after all, that *is* what those border towns in Mexico are known for. It's not like it's not true."

In return, Silvia asked, "And who made it that way? Whose money has shaped what those towns have become?"

The group ended up talking over dinner about the ways people impact one another's lives, discussing the repercussions of the power we exercise for good or evil in the ways we spend our money. Problems like prostitution, drug and human trafficking exist only because there are people willing to pay for them.

There's a familiar line of thinking that excuses a person's behavior based on their personal perception of "not hurting anyone." There is rarely any community strength or resilience built by actions that aim for such a low standard. We need to see the wildly beneficial possibilities of genuinely caring about our neighbors, and set our ambitions higher. When we are wise enough to recognize the interconnectedness of our lives, we begin to recognize as well how our choices, both big and small, impact the lives of others and contribute to the ultimate weakness or strength of our communities and nations.

One Day at a Time

"A skill like waking to an alarm clock might take a typical person a few days to master. For Luke, it took a few months. Luke is persistent: one day at a time."

When my sister Karen was 26 years old, many of her basic expectations for life were completely altered. The day after Luke was born, the pediatrician came into her hospital room to tell her he had Down syndrome. The quote above is the subtitled text that plays over the opening scene of the 12-minute documentary that was Luke's senior project at Whittier High School. He made *Journey to Independence* with Karen and his stepfather, Craig. Used by doctors, teachers and therapists, it's been a source of encouragement to many people around the world who are related to or know people with Down syndrome.

In the days that followed Luke's birth, Karen grieved the loss of what she had thought her life as a mother would be. She felt stunned by the number of challenges and responsibilities ahead. Overwhelmed with sorrow and questions, her heart searching to find her way, she felt a clear and peaceful answer rise up, "Take it one day at a time. You only have to do one day at a time."

It's a familiar refrain for many who have found help in personal recovery through Alcoholics Anonymous and other 12-step programs, but for Karen, the unfamiliar idea of doing life one day at a time was a fresh and workable concept. In those early days with Luke, she learned a new perspective and way of living. At first, Luke simply needed what all babies need, to be held, loved and nurtured. Help came from friends and new acquaintances day by day: a mother who knew how to assist babies who were slow to nurse, people willing to provide meals, and a social worker who enrolled Karen in a class for parents and children facing challenges. The stories of daily provision and help have continued through the years.

In the first scene of Luke's senior project, he gets out of bed at 5:44 am and crosses the dark room to turn off his alarm before beginning a typical day. As the short film proceeds we see Luke's system for getting himself dressed, how he makes himself breakfast, and how he accomplishes many other normal life skills like riding a bike, going to the YMCA to swim before going to school, doing laundry, walking his dog and hanging out at the movies with his buddy, Jace. Skills many of us can do without thinking and take for granted took years for Karen and Luke's friends, mentors, teachers, aids and family to help him accomplish.

What's easy for one person may be challenging for the next. Some people don't seem to recognize that's true for each of us. All of us have both strengths and weaknesses. The strengths that are most important to resilience are ones of character. Overall, we determine by our choices whether we will contribute to or detract from the whole of community life with our unique attributes, skills and abilities.

In school, some call these differences learning disabilities. I have many friends who simply endured their years of education, feeling stupid or slow because only particular strengths were acknowledged. There is no test that adequately assesses our value, worth or positive impact.

Luke had an interest in acting. With a lot of help from his support group, he was able to audition for and get a part on the television show, *Glee*. In a similar way, for Luke to continue to perform his basic life skills, he requires ongoing support and encouragement from those who want that for him. That kind of support takes daily, Herculean effort. For Luke and many others who face mental and physical obstacles, and certainly for their caregivers, "one day at a time" continues to be a necessary theme for achieving daily success and overall resilience.

The café lights came on overhead as the sun sank over the ocean in Carpenteria. Craig's family and friends took turns at the microphone, telling stories about good times they had shared with him and other ways his life had touched theirs. After a nine-month battle with cancer, Karen's husband, Craig, died in February 2017.

Because of her own journey through many other difficult times, Karen knew that she wanted to host a party in Craig's honor at a restaurant on the coast so that his extended family and community could gather to love, comfort and support each other. That night, with the sound of the surf in our ears, we shared dinner as the children played on the lawn around us. A slideshow of happy and memorable times had been set up by his sons Nikolai and Bradley, and looped on a big screen. There were handcrafted arrangements of succulents in whimsical containers provided by a friend. Each table had river-smoothed rocks and permanent markers so that we could all draw a picture or share some words, so our family gardens could have a place of remembering Craig.

When Karen spoke about the sorrow of Craig's illness and death, she reminded us again of the gift she received through Luke's birth and the necessity of learning that life was best lived taking one day at a time. She talked about being grateful for the present moment and for family and friends. Her gift to all of us that night was the opportunity to be together, to laugh and begin to create new memories.

Karen is one of the most resilient people I know. She sets aside time to make plans and takes action to build her strength and fortitude and have something to offer the people in her life. There are many kinds of challenges all of us face and many different things that can diminish our strength and love. It's important that we intentionally encourage and fortify ourselves and others in a variety of ways as we experience hard circumstances. Those choices ultimately build a strong sense of community and resilience.

Psychosis or Sanity?

"How many of you believe in God?" The professor placed air quotes around God, probably to signify the designation could be loosely assumed. A majority of the class tentatively raised a hand, me among them.

I was sitting in a classroom on the second floor of the Psychology building, ready to begin my last statistics class in grad school when our professor posed this question. I don't remember much from that introductory lecture, but the first few minutes left a lasting impression.

The class had about thirty students, and after the professor had elicited our responses, he leaned back on the edge of his desk and with arms folded said, "How many of you believe you can talk to God in some way... maybe prayer?"

Again the air quotes, now around prayer. Some of the same hands lifted more slowly. Like most students, I think we were beginning to recognize a classic "set up," wondering how he was going to spin our answers to these questions, likely to illustrate our ignorance of statistics.

"How many of you believe that God actually hears what you say, hears what you pray?" A number of hands rose with perceptible reluctance and the professor made a comment about how that type of response, believing in a god who listens to people, might merit a clinical note in a patient assessment. He got a chuckle.

"Now, how many of you believe you can hear God speaking to you?" I looked around, and seeing I was the only student with a hand in the air on that one, steeled myself for the expected shaming "take down" familiar to students.

"Good to see only one of you hears voices." The professor drew the expected laughs at my expense and continued to make a few points about delusions, hallucinations and possible psychosis in a case presenting like mine. Relatively secure I was sane and functional, I recall trying to take the ribbing good-naturedly and participating in the discussions that followed. But obviously, I also remember it because it hurt. It's similar to attitudes I still encounter, and I've come to recognize that air quotes are probably a good idea, not because of skepticism but because we're all talking about a concept that mostly defies description: God.

Having grown up the way I did with the opportunity to know amazing people who demonstrated nitty-gritty, authentic faith in their daily lives, I've often been puzzled by how dismissive others have been of my perspective. I was taught that God is Love and shown what that can look like. Not that love was demonstrated perfectly or without hypocrisy, only that the values, principles and concepts of faith in God entered my life with "skin on," so to speak.

People insist that it's impossible or crazy to listen for God's voice inside that tells us there's a higher way that's more loving than we're naturally inclined to be. I'm reminded of a favorite line from a favorite movie. Inigo

Montoya, in *Princess Bride*, classically states, "You keep using that word. I do not think it means what you think it means." Our definitions of God are especially diverse and fraught with personal content that make normal conversation and respectful dialogue extremely difficult. It's important we take the time to listen and understand. If ever there was a topic with nuances that require superior listening skills, "God" is surely up there on the list.

Finding the solutions to the challenges of our age requires us to make fewer assumptions about each other and to listen for the content our words are trying to carry in the context of our stories of development. Before we discourse in any depth, we may need to figure out if we're even talking about the same things and not disregard the other out of hand because we assume we all know what we mean and what we're talking about.

When we were working on the challenges of the Katrina recovery, circumstances in Louisiana really took a toll on our lives, and by the middle of 2006, Graeme and I found our personal operating systems in need of a serious reboot of some kind.

Thankfully, our friends Gem and Alan were trying something new and invited us to a weekend retreat they were leading at the old Mission in Santa Barbara. Graeme and I went, finding in the quiet the fresh perspective we needed to keep going. Graeme, in particular, found a deeper understanding for himself about the interior quiet and listening mind required to solve problems and work toward peaceful resolutions. He still references those hours of stillness spent on the beach during the retreat as a philosophical turning point.

While we were working on the recovery for Hurricane Harvey in 2017, we were encouraged by Gem's and Alan's podcast, *Unhurried Living,* as they shared the meditative practices of William Wilberforce, Martin Luther King, Jr., and Mother Teresa, all people who dealt with immense challenges in the world with compassion and fortitude.

Gem and Alan shared a list of ten commitments King tried to fulfill each day. He asked the same of others. The commitments were both sublime desires, such as "Meditate daily on the teachings and life of Jesus," as well as admonitions to basic practical actions, such as "Observe with both friend and foe, the ordinary rules of courtesy."

Wilberforce, the statesman who was instrumental in ending England's slave trade, wrote, "I am persuaded that to withdraw the mind one day in seven from its ordinary trains of thought and passion, and to occupy it in contemplating subjects of a higher order, which by their magnitude make worldly interests sink into littleness, has the happiest effect on the intellectual and moral system."[3]

We could all be improved by Wilberforce's "happiest effect" on our reasoning abilities. Just take a quick scroll through social media if you need convincing. I don't think it's a sign of psychosis to say that we would do better if we were all listening for the voice of love. Our ability to truly hear each other and work together is essential and greatly helped by taking the time to enjoy a place of quiet within ourselves.

---

[3] Murray Andrew Pura, Vital Christianity: The Life and Spirituality of William Wilberforce (Biography), (Christian Focus; Revised edition (November 20, 2003)) 60-61.

One Name Doesn't Fit All

There was a preacher on the radio as I was growing up who sounded to me like the cartoon character, Huckleberry Hound. Hearing his voice one time on our drive home from school prompted my mom to tell us the story of how, on a Sunday night during the Depression when money was especially tight in the nation, her dad decided to play hooky from the Baptist meeting and go have a listen to this preacher friend.

Mom's family came into the service and quietly took a seat in a back pew. Sharing a similar sense of humor with my granddad, when Preacher J. Vernon McGee noticed them, he stopped and boomed from his Presbyterian pulpit, "Hallelujah, folks! We're going to have a big offering tonight! The Baptists are in the house!" From family stories like this, the legacy of relaxed friendships across religious boundaries became a value I unknowingly held as well.

I grew up attending a Congregational church, and my parents' friendships easily included others from a spectrum of Christian faith, such as Baptists, Assembly of God, Methodists, Four Square, Nazarenes, Mennonites,

Episcopalians, Quakers, and Catholics. We also had friends within our community of other faiths and grew up learning to be respectful and interested in our differences. We enjoyed the chance to find out what we had in common, usually on occasions that involved food, celebration and good humor.

While most people acknowledge the obvious fallacy that all Americans share a common identity, it's surprising how often in different forms of media and entertainment people of various nationalities, ethnicities and faiths are referred to as though they are a single entity with a united, singular set of values, political will, and social agenda.

I can speak from my heritage as a Christian and point out the innumerable and various theological positions existing amongst those who are called by the one word, "Christian." Other words like "evangelical" that seem to be more specific fail to clarify murky waters that hide individuals and their personal journeys of faith. Many of the distinctions between Catholics, Protestants, denominations and sects came about as the result of centuries of hostility and painful divisions due to strong convictions and differences of opinion. Christians throughout history have been known to punish and even kill each other over these disputes.

From my perspective, the same is true within other religions as well. Many faiths that are identified by the same overarching name often have many powerful points of disagreement between the orders within them and each person within those. We simply cannot move forward in productive dialogue with a conviction that labels or stereotypes of any sort are adequate for understanding one another or the issues confronting us.

While it might be easier or seem expedient to do life by color code or brand, identifying people's personal beliefs, intentions, and behavior this way does not work. We were made for relational understanding developed by personal interactions and experiences. It's only by cultivating relationship that we truly grow to understand people and can hope to become wise in the way of human connections.

Stranger Danger

Phil had given me a lift home from high school one afternoon and we were sitting in his car with the windows down under the big camphor tree hanging over the street, talking about an upcoming school project. My neighbor Mrs. Green, our genial and protective grandmotherly presence across the street, stepped out on her porch and shook her head, waving in a backhanded sweeping motion, silently telling Phil to move along.

I stepped out from the passenger side and waved over the roof of the car to let her see that I was there as well. She threw her hands up angrily, turned on her heel and went back inside. We both knew that she had disapproved of us sitting and talking in the car, a black boy and white girl. As I got back in to sit down, it was obvious we both felt deflated.

Phil was a year ahead of me in school; I respected him and was glad for his friendship. We were from similar families. His mom and mine stayed home raising younger siblings. His dad was a professor at Fuller Seminary and my dad was an administrator at Jet Propulsion Lab. Our families attended church and volunteered in the community. We were both good students, enjoyed playing different sports and had a lot of friends in common.

Phil offered, "She thinks she's right about making me move along. She thinks she's keeping her home safe." Phil's tone of compassion and effort to see how she might be viewing things made an impression on me. "You know," he said, "I think the most dangerous prejudices are the ones we don't even know we have."

That stuck with me, the thought that I might have dangerous prejudices myself. I learned that day to question the assumptions I make about people. I need to give my attitudes a second, open-hearted look and be open to other's observations. It helped to hear Phil say the same applied to him. His dad had paved the way in being willing to wrestle with the contradictions of character that surface around race. Dr. William Pannell had written a controversial book, *My Friend The Enemy,* and had been one of the founders of what would become a center named after him for African American studies at the seminary. Phil and his family were deep thinkers when it came to what keeps people from connecting.

It's not simply stereotyping that's the problem. Some stereotyping is obviously useful, in the sense that we're able to predict behavior and adapt to our environments. For instance, "all 5-year-olds need supervision" or "16-year-olds are just learning to drive" are stereotypes that can help us.

But, if we feel something automatic and negative about someone we don't know and are willing to admit to it, we're actually at the starting place for our own personal growth. Being willing to recognize an unfounded assumption may develop into the more mature ability to consider another point of view.

I don't think I'm being overly optimistic about my neighbor Mrs. Green when I say she would have liked Phil and discovered they had a lot in common, in spite of a fifty-year age gap and being different colors. For years, she kept a watchful eye on our house, generously shared her baking with us, and was a caring older presence in my mom's life. I'm convinced now that her heart would have won out if I had tried to get her to see the light. But I was young, annoyed and impatient.

If she had taken the time to get to know Phil, she would have found he had an artist's eye as a photographer and an interest in her work as a potter. He would have enjoyed seeing her work on the wheel in her back studio. She had an obvious desire to be affirmed for her creations and appreciated anyone who took an interest. They might have become great friends. I could have taken the time to help Mrs. Green question her assumptions.

I have a sign over my kitchen sink that says, "Don't believe everything you think." I like that. It's a good place to start.

As a child, I remember hearing that our Ugandan friend Festo had been staying at another friend's home in nearby San Marino, a mostly white community. Wanting to take a break from the writing he was doing, he had taken a walk around the block, only to be picked up by the police and taken back to his friend's home. The police wanted reassurance that he had a "right" to be there. This accomplished man who had traveled the planet, met with world leaders and shared the pulpit with Billy Graham was suspect simply because he wanted to stretch his legs. Festo handled the incident with his usual grace and forgiveness, but it was wrong that he was seen as a threat and treated as such only because of his skin color.

In high school, one of the guys from the basketball team came to social science class upset about being pulled over the night before on his way home from practice. He related how he had been made to get out of the car, lie on the ground face down, spread eagle without any reason or explanation. He hadn't done anything wrong and was churning about having been treated as if he had. Our white male teacher used the class time for discussion. He asked about our different experiences with the police. I remember being grateful as he highlighted how we seemed to have had hostile or friendly encounters with the sheriffs and police departments in our area, primarily based on our skin color, not whether we were good or bad students, straight-laced or rowdy. That day helped solidify my conviction that presumed innocence was more readily assumed about folks who looked like me.

Judging people's insides by the color of their outsides doesn't work. We've all experienced people who have been dismissive when challenged about prejudice. It takes a certain amount of maturity to recognize the biases we each have that are hindering our individual and collective progress. It requires honest work to discover where our mistaken beliefs and opinions about others originated and address them and calibrate them to the positive virtues and values we esteem. It's vital we stop seeing one another through our unconscious filters. We need to be able to move past our natural "stranger danger" perceptions of in-groups and out-groups. It's from our identity as a united nation built of individuals who value our differences and interdependency that we'll be able to determine our best ways forward.

Safe Sanctuary

My sister Linda was living in South Central Los Angeles in 1992, working as a middle school teacher at the time the Los Angeles riots broke out. When the police officers accused of using excessive force in the arrest of Rodney King were acquitted with what many felt was an unjust verdict, people took to the streets, directing their anger and outrage against individuals and businesses that had nothing to do with the court decision.

I was able to spend time on the phone with Linda over the days of the unrest as she and three other teachers stayed inside their home with doors locked and shades pulled. I was surprised by Linda's sense of peace. She had been living in the neighborhood for more than a year at that point, and while she was aware of rioting close by and could see a gas station on fire from her bedroom window, she felt relatively safe because she was convinced that the majority of her neighbors were law-abiding people who wanted the hostility to end and their lives to return to normal. Living in the community, walking the few blocks to work each day, getting to know her middle school students and their families, had given Linda a more multi-dimensional view of South Central Los Angeles than the one portrayed in television news.

One afternoon some months before, Linda had been walking a few blocks from her home when she saw a pack of rowdy teenage boys she didn't know turn the corner at the other end of the street onto the sidewalk she was on. Her heart began to race and she debated about turning back the way she had just come or continuing toward the group, hoping they would let her pass without incident. She heard a noise nearby and was relieved to see one of her students and his mother on their front porch, waving Linda into the safety of their home. The neighbor saw Linda's vulnerability and offered her sanctuary until the guys had moved on.

As a mother, I've learned to see the world through the lens of family relationships. At heart, we are a world made up of mothers, fathers, sons, daughters, sisters, brothers, grandfathers, grandmothers, aunts and uncles. By and large, we are people who love and care for our families and desire good for ourselves and for each other. While there are people in the world whose actions make life difficult and painful for others, there are many more who work to behave like the human sisters and brothers we are, aware of our intrinsic similarities and interconnectedness. Together, by choosing one simple act of kindness after another, we can collectively make our neighborhoods safer and more hospitable for all of us.

Ugly Americans

"You call this a steak?" The older couple seated a few tables away were being loud and disapproving. Graeme and I cringed in embarrassment. We were backpacking in Europe for a few weeks in 1982, and this small restaurant in Paris was our anniversary splurge. Like us, the other couple were Americans and unable to speak French. Unlike us, they seemed to think that their difficulty in understanding the waiter was his fault. To hear these other Americans tell it, a steak in France couldn't possibly compare to a steak from their home state "in the U.S. of A." I wanted to speak up but was uncertain what to say. I was certain that was no way for Americans abroad to behave.

Five years earlier, after my first year in college, I had traveled to Europe with one of my former teachers, Sylvia Jones. She called to tell me during my freshman year in college that she was taking a group of high school students on a backpacking trip to some of her favorite destinations, and asked if I could join them.

Sylvia had been my German teacher, but I'd learned much more from her than language during the three years I was her student and the years we stayed in touch afterward. I gained a larger perspective through our friendship. Sylvia had grown up on the campus of the historically black AMN College in Arkansas where her father taught German and French. She stayed and attended college there and went on to study for a time in Paris, where she perfected her French. She was extremely talented. I remember her flawless performance of an aria from the opera *Porgy and Bess* for our John Muir High assembly. She was fascinated by different cultures, loved history, enjoyed all kinds of music and was a gourmet cook.

Sylvia actively worked to pass along her enjoyment of the world to her students. That summer in college, we spent over six weeks exploring France, Germany, East Germany, Austria and Switzerland. We traveled with train passes and mostly stayed in youth hostels. Our budget was about ten dollars a day (per person), and Sylvia made those dollars perform miracles.

One of the most meaningful moments on that trip was spent together visiting Dachau, the World War II Nazi concentration camp. As we walked through Dachau looking at horrifying pictures of countless starved and naked bodies stacked like firewood, Sylvia reminded us of the importance of understanding history to keep from repeating it.

We also traveled to East Germany, past the wall in Berlin. To reach West Berlin from West Germany in 1977, we had to travel by train through the restrictive, socialist country of East Germany. West Berlin sat as an isolated island in the middle of a hostile state. Walking through Checkpoint Charlie as a group of young black and white Americans caused a buzz of unintelligible discussion among the border guards.

We stayed in a youth hostel inside the Olympic stadium in West Berlin, where Mack Robinson, one of our high school alumni, had won the silver medal for the 200-meter race, and Jesse Owens won four gold medals in 1936 during Hitler's Nazi regime. Sylvia helped us better understand this part of history, recounting the powerful symbolism of Mack's and Jesse's accomplishments for the United States and humanity during the Jim Crow era. In the face of opposition, experiencing immense challenges and a lack of official recognition, these men represented the best in all of us.

Additionally, in many of the places we traveled in Europe we were not simply accommodated but given extra attention and made welcome. Vernon, Sylvia's husband and an aerospace scientist, joined us for some of the trip, bringing along their young son and daughter. Looking back, we were an unusual group of Americans—black and white, adults and children, college and high school students.

From our last evening in Europe, I retain a magical impression of Sylvia's joyful interactions in her fluent French with the wait staff as we feasted together at an excellent restaurant in Paris. I remember being treated with sweeping hospitality. The chef sent out special dishes for us to try, on the house, and eventually came from the kitchen with some of the other staff to join us at our large table on the balcony as the restaurant slowed down for the night. They simply wanted to be with us. Actually, they wanted to be with Sylvia, who made room for many others in her circle of joy. The food was exceptional, beyond anything we'd ever experienced, but it was people around the table who created the extraordinary memory.

I recently renewed my friendship with one of the other girls from that trip, Felicia. She reminded me that Sheila and I surprised her with cake and candles on her 16th birthday during our travels. It was great to see Felicia for the first time since our adventure, all grown up, a chemist at Caltech. It was interesting to find out how similarly we remembered that evening of feasting, as though it was a scene lifted from a favorite movie viewed over and over, the crowning point of a well-told story where unlikely friends have arrived at journey's end to spend a last evening celebrating their camaraderie.

There's a stark contrast in my mind's eye between that memorable night with Sylvia and the tense atmosphere in the restaurant a few years later as Graeme and I tried to celebrate our anniversary. When people choose to enjoy the good in each moment with gratitude, sharing their encouraging opinions and displaying an interest in what others have to offer, they increase their own happiness, enhance the lives of others and unwittingly contribute to greater understanding between cultures and nations.

The America the World Sees

"Wait a minute, all of you are traveling together? Where did you say you were from again?"

I recall a conversation in a German youth hostel on that trip in 1977. A number of European and Australian students wanted to know more about our integrated group and our lives in America. Our friendships seemed to present a puzzle to them.

As we all talked, they offered their impressions, gleaned from the news they had grown up with in their home countries, that white and black Americans were never friends with each other, especially in cities like Los Angeles. They mentioned the Watts Riots and different Civil Rights-era news. They knew nothing of the progress we were making and the types of integration stories those like us were living. I recall feeling disappointed that who I thought we were at heart wasn't visible to other countries.

Individuals and groups who practice selfish, self-seeking entitlement and hostility toward others can come from any nation, ethnicity, religion or socio-economic group. Happily, so can individuals who act on behalf of others, caring about people the way they want to be cared for themselves.

We often only hear other nations' bad news. The same is true within our countries. What usually makes the news are those events we consider problems, but they're not always balanced with the stories that describe how culture is working and making progress. This can be improved by deliberately focusing attention on those things that positively address our challenges and increase our community strength. News coverage should more frequently seek out the stories that inform us and help us make the connections that mend the tears in our social fabric. This mindset encourages us to find new ways to bridge the divides that separate us.

The same is evident after disaster. It's not unusual for media coverage to seek out and emphasize destruction. It makes for interesting pictures and satisfies a voyeuristic desire for excitement. Sometimes the camera reveals controversy and criminal behavior. While there's value in helping viewers understand the extent of damage caused by an event and in warning the public about those who may take advantage of disastrous circumstances, being diligent to continue coverage over the long haul of the real challenges faced by survivors and the effort required to rebuild empowers the recovery process.

We will be better equipped for our next disaster if we have been shown accurate news and information about the last one. We will have learned from the wisdom of others' journeys through disaster and from the intervention and analysis of those working on the event. When news media helps our nation focus on the priorities of both response and recovery, pointing out those actions that inspire us to greater compassion as a community, the positive impacts will be immeasurable.

207

The Best Kind of Pyramid Scheme

Shortly after college, I was working with the Mental Health Association of Los Angeles County (MHALA) on a workbook intended for elementary age children called *The Mental Health Youth Award*. The concept was to create a positive way for kids to learn about mental health. My colleague Bev and I developed simple activities, listening to input from a large variety of advisors from organizations around Los Angeles. Given the diverse opinions about mental health and how best to introduce the topic to children, it's a wonder the project was completed and had the measure of success it attained.

One of the activities we created for the workbook involved filling in squares arranged in a pyramid with one box at the top, two in the next row, three in the third, and four boxes as the base. Titled, "Values," the idea was to get the kids thinking about how their priorities and the things they valued shaped their behavior. I recall sitting in the MHALA conference room with many of the advisors as we discussed the wording. A few of us felt strongly that what went in that top box was key to mental health and we proposed that the activity instructions suggest strong, powerful words about human character for that number-one slot, like love or kindness.

Others disagreed and insisted that no ideas were better or worse for a top value or priority. The committee's decision is reflected in this line from that activity, "Although you may have different ideas than your friends and family, it's important to recognize that their ideas are neither better nor worse, just different." And while I agree that each person has the right to decide what is most important to them, I am still persuaded that when individuals choose values like money, sex, power or fame as their number-one priority, their personal mental health will suffer, as well as our strength and resilience as a community. By choosing to value such characteristics as love or kindness in our top box, we're better off both individually and communally.

Words are containers for meaning. Understanding what particular words hold for each other is useful in creating dialogue. This task of gaining insight into the meaning of the words we use, and in particular, the meanings of love and kindness, will be helped by telling our stories, sharing our life experiences and acknowledging the people—the mother, father, teacher, grandparent, friend or sibling—who demonstrated something of this highest value to us.

Other languages evidently offer more options when talking about different kinds of love, having distinct words for love between friends, sexual love, love for a family member, love of chocolate, love for country or love of a cause. Love obviously has a lot of different meanings in different contexts, and seeking to value compassion as a culture will require the contribution of our many different perspectives.

I learned in Sunday school that one of the best definitions of love came from a poetic passage in 1 Corinthians describing charity, an Old English word for love. There was a rhythm of both positive and negative characteristics: Love is patient and kind, not envious or boastful. Love isn't arrogant or rude; it doesn't insist on getting its own way. Love isn't angry, touchy or reactive. Love doesn't meditate on evil. Love doesn't celebrate wickedness, but when truth wins everyone wins. Love is able to bear anything. Love always believes, always hopes, and is able to endure anything. Love never fails. That same passage insists that without love even the greatest human or supernatural accomplishment won't ring true. Love is the essential ingredient.

Recognizing and learning to walk in love is a lifelong journey. Sometimes we're taught by first experiencing the negative. That was true for my friend Toni Gilyard. A poem in her book, *The Girl Between the Trees*, illustrates the discoveries we acquire from hard experience:

If it's forced
If it's measured
If it's required or bargained

If it's earned
If it's withheld
If it's rewarded or restricted
haunted or twisted

If it's controlled or coerced
If it is anything... it is anything
But Love

If we want to experience vibrant community life and resilience , we need to be able to talk together without censure or ridicule about our true values and priorities. Talking together about who we are, how we came to think the way we do and why we are convinced of our particular opinions is a formidable beginning. In spite of our many differences, those kinds of conversations will start to connect us. When we are connected, we'll be able to see the many ways the highest values can be implemented in our day-to-day lives and used to strengthen our built infrastructure.

Compatibility Over Competition

I was home in Sacramento days after having Braden, and watched the news with dismay as a neighborhood fire turned into the Oakland Firestorm. It began in October of 1991 and marks a place in disaster history because of the huge devastation and the lessons learned.

One of the more tragic aspects of this event was that fire companies from other areas arriving to help were obstructed, not just by the steep terrain and narrow roads but by equipment incompatibility. It turned out not all their hose couplings fit the hydrants in the Oakland hills. Similarly, communication between different responders was hampered by mismatched radio frequencies.

As a result of these difficulties, California developed the Standardized Emergency Management System to facilitate cooperation, communication and compatibility of equipment between different jurisdictions in the event of large-scale disasters. Eventually, the Department of Homeland Security established a similar program in 2004, the National Incident Management System, to enable cooperation between all those responding to an event.

These important systems represent an underlying philosophy we must have as a nation. Our geopolitical boundaries serve us better when we recognize our interconnectedness. Certainly there are many considerations that need to be addressed, but we must be able to function cooperatively across these various borders with our neighbors wherever and whenever possible. Human-constructed boundaries, whether between cities, counties, states or nations, become less relevant during disasters. When we are challenged by forces outside our control, it's our connections that are most important.

We would do well as a nation to apply the same concepts to everything that would profit from standardizing systems for compatibility instead of competition. We need to care more about the *purpose* of systems and organizations and their impacts on the people they're meant to serve. We have been in areas of the country where new housing construction is so segmented that it's impossible to walk, ride a bike or drive directly from one part of town to another. Neighborhoods are literally walled off from one another. While this is irritating on a day-to-day basis, it makes simple interaction between neighborhoods difficult. It also becomes a critical obstacle during disaster response. If there are only limited ways to commute from one part of town to another, imagine how much more difficult this becomes during a crisis.

While we take many aspects of daily life for granted, we need to begin to look to the big picture. Our well-developed concepts of competitiveness and so-called "success" are not sufficient for resilience. It is important we recognize and take action on the many ways cooperation is the wiser course for sustaining and improving our community life, and one that will position us for a stronger future.

215

Lice, Lunch Boxes and a Handgun

I was sitting on the edge of the bathtub in sloppy wet workout clothes, whisper-yelling to the other room, trying to stop 4-year-old Ryan from making another noisy jump off the upper bunk. I was vainly hoping he wouldn't wake up the baby from a nap until I had once again finished using a fine-toothed comb to examine every last follicle of my first-grader's wet hair. I was doing all I could to rid our household of lice for the third time that year.

It had been a rough year for us at our neighborhood elementary school. Andrew was behind in reading, writing and math, perhaps because he had had a hard time concentrating in his class of 35 students. As we were able to, several of us mothers volunteered in the classroom to help the overloaded teacher, but it wasn't enough to keep that group of students on course. Plus, the school couldn't afford playground supervisors during recess and lunchtime. For Andrew, that meant being pushed around a lot and having his lunch boxes and thermoses broken by older boys using them to play keep away.

One second-grade boy at school had been especially rough on Andrew and had repeatedly singled him out at lunchtime, trying to control how Andrew played. Andrew didn't want to keep getting shoved around. I had tried talking with his teacher and other staff to take action on what I thought was unacceptable behavior and had set up play dates with the boy's mother at their home and ours so the children could hang out and all of us could get to know each other. But still, what was happening on campus continued to concern me. The day before this third discovery of head lice, when picking up Andrew, I found out that the boy who had been bullying him had brought a handgun to school.

Standing around with staff and some parents, trying to understand what had happened, I learned the boy had pulled the gun out of his backpack either to scare or "just impress" other students. The gun had been confiscated by a teacher and the boy's parents called in. Of course, I was concerned. As I stood there, holding the baby with the other two tugging on me to leave, I asked if there would be a school meeting to talk about it. School needed to be a safer place for our kids. The general consensus was dismissive. After all, the student would be suspended for a few days for bringing his father's gun to school. One especially disparaging remark came from the principal, "Now, Mom. That gun wasn't loaded."

I recognize now that my experiences in high school of being bullied and exposed to violence were influencing my strong feelings about things like class size, playground supervision, and the need for a zero-tolerance policy on bullying at this elementary school. Added to that, as it was the spring of 1992, my perspective was influenced by my sister's experiences living and working in South Central Los Angeles.

I felt as though I could see biases in the way things were being handled at Andrew's school. Although I couldn't articulate it as a young mother, I saw things differently than the principal, staff and apparently many of the other parents in our white, middle-class neighborhood. The child who had been causing difficulty for Andrew and had brought the gun from home was white. His father owned a business a few blocks from the school, and his mother was frequently on campus volunteering and picking up her children. They were community insiders. This situation, a second-grader showing off with a handgun wasn't perceived as a possible threat because of certain cultural assumptions being made. I wasn't suggesting a stronger punishment or anything that would have shamed or belittled the child. I wanted to be part of the dialogue and decision-making process to address what I saw as a serious problem—a lack of effective, compassionate adult guidance and influence on the campus.

In hindsight, I can see many ways I could have communicated and advocated better. At the time I only felt as though my role as a concerned mom seemed insufficient for me to be considered an informed, relevant voice. I learned that not all stakeholders are routinely included in the significant decisions that impact them, especially those people who are considered by a system to be without authority or status. In this case, I felt others were perceiving my qualifications and experience solely being defined and limited by the fact that I was holding a baby and wrangling two energetic boys.

In the months following these incidents, I was heartened to learn about another mother whose opinions had been respected and even lauded in a crisis. I was hearing from friends in Southern California that they had been encouraged by the authoritative image Dr. Lucy Jones presented during TV interviews just after the Landers earthquake. Lucy, a seismologist, was answering reporters' questions at the Seismology Lab at Caltech when her husband, also a seismologist, was needed to resolve a computer issue. While Lucy was on camera, he came and handed off one of their sons.

That day, during a disaster, Lucy's role as a mother was seen as an additional strength and professional attribute. As she continued to calmly and knowledgeably speak about the earthquake's magnitude and expected aftershocks, she casually held her son and broke long-held prejudices and stereotypes that one role negates the other. She was perceived as reassuring, and the presence of her child was not counted by other professionals as a detriment to her intelligence, insights and role as an expert. People I talked with in Los Angeles found her interview comforting. Lucy has humorously said that her male colleagues could have said the exact same thing, but people seem to feel better when Mommy says it's okay.

We're all inclined to prejudice, stereotypes and assumptions, and we must recognize this as lower-level, reactive reasoning. We need to realize that many people have worthwhile contributions that belong in our decision-making process, regardless of their role or appearance. This is especially true in the midst of crises. But, it's also true in our day-to-day lives. Resilient people are adaptable, question their assumptions and quickly recognize their own misconceptions and biases.

A Love of Learning

In the summer of 1992, as my sister's community in Los Angeles tried to piece their neighborhoods and businesses back together after the Los Angeles riots, I began looking for other school options after Andrew's challenging first-grade year. What I really wanted was the simplicity of keeping my boys in the school a few blocks from our home. But at the time, I just didn't have it in me to send Andrew, along with his younger brother, Ryan, back to circumstances that seemed a risk to their safety.

We didn't make the lottery at the charter school. We were put at the bottom of a long wait list at the local Catholic school. We looked at the commutes to other schools in the area and determined they were just too far away to make full participation possible, not to mention the question of how we would swing the costs of private education. I felt dismayed as I realized I was out of options. Just before school started, someone suggested homeschooling. I looked into it as best I could (prior to the days of internet resources) and became a very reluctant homeschool mom. I was unconvinced homeschooling was a legitimate form of education, but fairly certain it was still the best choice for us that fall in 1992.

I had never seen myself as a teacher. Like many moms, I had looked forward to sending my kids to school and getting back to my career interests in mental health. But, if I was going to be their teacher, I was going to do it right, God help them. My first days of homeschooling had us all up, dressed, fed and saluting the flag in our front hall every morning at 8 o'clock. Similar to the traditional schoolmarm of old, I used a big, erasable whiteboard to teach the boys their letters and numbers, and gave them the privilege of doing their exercises on it when they behaved. They had a small table they shared for a desk, and I gave them worksheets to fill out. I measured my success or failure by how much we covered in their textbooks each week.

I was often frustrated by the way caring for the baby, housework, shopping, cooking and all of their playful energy kept us from making progress the way I expected. When we temporarily moved to Los Angeles in March 1994 to work on the recovery for the Northridge Earthquake, I wanted my teaching days to come to an end. But continuing to homeschool seemed the best choice for the boys since we would be returning to Sacramento well after the school year started in the fall.

As our move to Los Angeles extended and finally became permanent, I continued to homeschool all three of my guys, mostly because their development and abilities ran at a different pace than the way testing and placement was happening in the schools—they were ahead on some fronts and woefully behind on others. I had images of my 11-year-old who couldn't seem to get the hang of reading, sitting knees to chest in a desk too small for him, having been placed in a first-grade class instead of a fifth.

Our lifestyle in Southern California began to soften our education routines. We went on hikes to make old English literature more interesting, carrying backpacks with books and snacks, reading by local waterfalls. We created salt maps of Egypt in the front yard and dug up the Rosetta stone in the back, making the geography of the world and ancient history more exciting. My friends, Sheri and Jody, both teachers before choosing to home-school, and living within walking distance of our house, formed a casual, organic structure of support for our three homeschooling families with thirteen children. Our circle would expand, depending on what subjects or events we were doing, to include many other women and students with plenty of socialization for the kids, the most frequently mentioned criticism of homeschooling.

There were also opportunities like the trip the five of us took with my parents, traveling economy style for several weeks on the East Coast, staying in motels, eating most of our meals as picnics assembled from a Styrofoam ice chest out of the back of our rented mini-van. We visited colonial sites, Revolutionary and Civil War battlefields, museums, the White House and Capitol, listening to relevant books on tape as we drove, and giving the whole family a context for American history, grounded in a sense of place.

By the time the guys were young teens, we had more outside educational options all over Southern California as homeschooling became more popular. They went to their biology course in a garage-turned-lab with a marine biologist-turned-homeschool mom, conducting 34 different dissections. A Caltech student, working on her doctorate, taught a chemistry class in her apartment's recreation room. The lectures and exhibits at the Huntington Library piqued the kids' interest in everything from European art to the artifacts of Abraham Lincoln's life and legacy. The Science Center, tours of Jet Propulsion Lab and free lectures at Caltech offered exposure to current scientific thought.

For me, the initially undesirable course of homeschooling that had seemed restrictive was unexpectedly liberating. I realized what a privilege it was to have this extra time with our sons, sharing our hearts, seeing them grow and develop their unique personalities and interests. I didn't determine that homeschooling was the superior educational choice for everyone, but rather came to see it as one respectable option among many. My homeschooling experience was similar to what I had been given growing up—family relationships, both private and public education, travel with a teacher who loved the world, a diversity of friendships and the joy of cultivating faith in love greater than our own.

Through many trials and lots of errors, I also discovered what I came to believe is the key to excellent education: teaching is best focused on creating within the heart of the student a love of learning and a willingness to grow. A person who continues to be open to learning and remains teachable throughout their lifetime is adaptable and strong and can contribute this same type of resilience to the relationships that enable healthy community life.

The Whole Is Cooler Than Some of Its Parts

"Hit it!" I yelled. My uncle pushed on the throttle; the ski boat leapt forward, pulling the rope taut and lifting me out of the water, my two skis bouncing unevenly, wind in my hair, water dripping from the life jacket.

"Thank God," I thought, "I'm up." Managing to keep my balance, I let go of the rope with one hand, grinned, and waved to Graeme, Keith and Karli in the boat. The rest of my extended family had somehow all become impressive skiers over years of summers spent together on Uncle Ken and Aunt Wanda's houseboat. I had not.

After a happy and uneventful trip around a portion of Lake Oroville, awkwardly cutting back and forth across the wake, I miscalculated. I fell forward, did a face plant, and forgetting to let go of the rope, continued in that posture long enough to push my contacts into the back of my eyeballs. As much as I would like to be cool and well-accomplished, there's ample evidence to the contrary, and little hope at this point that I will suddenly pull it off.

For instance, while I like unexpectedly meeting and renewing friendships with past classmates or colleagues, recognizing them has posed a problem. In the past, on more than one occasion, I've been caught asking well-known celebrities, "Hey, don't I know you? Didn't we go to high school together?"

My kids still joke, "Hey Mom, there's a celebrity! Want to go ask if you went to high school with each other?"

I may be slow but I know better than to say it out loud now. Still, I've found fresh ways to reveal my lack of cool. Information I know one minute can go missing in the next, as though someone hid the file folder on my desk.

I was working in the garden one day when my neighbor, Tiffany, came over and asked if I wanted to go to a party with her. One of the clients where she worked was performing: Tom Petty. I said, "Who?" She named some songs, nothing pulling up the file that should have been handy. She looked visibly relieved when the time didn't work for me.

At our friends' wedding, the bride, Lacey, and a bunch of girlfriends were dancing up a storm to a song I didn't know. I turned to my friend Stevie Harrell and commented, "What a fun song! What is it?"

She responded with an odd half-smile, "*Single Ladies*, by Beyoncé ."

I smiled, said I liked it and kept bobbing to the rhythm as we watched our kids goof around. In the following days, I noticed the song playing at the mall, in restaurants, and the grocery store and felt profoundly uncool for being so far out of the loop. It wasn't until the Grammy nominations were announced the next year that I realized how cosmically out of it I really was. Stevie's husband, Kuk Harrell, was a producer on *Single Ladies*. He won a Grammy for it.

Thankfully, my friends and family care more about me than whether or not I'm cool. We are not part of a high school clique. We don't believe we need to be the same or even similar to form a friendship. We don't need to look like or dress like each other. We don't care whether we went to Ivy League schools, community colleges or if we attended college at all. There is not an up or down based on salary or lifestyle. We don't compare our neighborhoods or houses or need to drive a certain class of car to accept each other. We don't think sharing the same opinions, politics or the same faith is required for circle membership. Frankly, many of us believe that having to agree with someone to be friends is a form of manipulation or control. Friendship comes from finding what we have in common, not from insisting that we believe the same things.

We've found that valuing and respecting each other is what's necessary. Resilient families, friends and neighbors make an effort to discover where connections exist and what it is about the other person that is remarkable. There is always something. We are each unique. We build strong communities from these foundations.

Shallow values will not suffice as the foundation of our social and cultural infrastructure that underlies the strength of America's built infrastructure—our buildings, bridges, roads, energy grids, health and education systems. The construction materials for the most safe, secure and strong infrastructure as a nation are found in our relationships with one another. Anything that alienates and divides us ultimately leaves us weak and exposed to disaster. Friendship and simple human compassion are more essential to our resilience than any other elements or characteristics.

Certainly, none of us needs to be some particular version of cool, attractive, intelligent, talented or educated to be resilient. We do, however, need to care. Let's knock off the shaming and one-upmanship that has become so common in our culture. It doesn't move us forward in the positive directions we need as a nation. Our variety of interests, our diverse life experiences, and our particular and innovative ways of thinking will make us strong as a whole. We need each other. There's a wise old adage, "The whole is greater than the sum of the parts." It really is.

What're You Lookin' At?

My snow skiing abilities rival my prowess on water skis. When I was in my teens, my Aunt Wanda and I took a skiing lesson together on a slope near Lake Tahoe in hopes of improving our skills. After receiving about thirty minutes of instruction on a lower hill, our instructor directed us to a ski lift, saying he'd evaluate what he could see of our skiing from the bottom. Reaching the top, Aunt Wanda and I congratulated each other on our ability to get off the chair without falling down or blocking other skiers coming up behind us. That was the high point of my run.

The next thing I knew, I was speeding downhill, horrified, out of control and unable to stop. The only part of the lesson I remembered on my plummet to the bottom was keeping my knees bent. Instead of cutting back and forth across the hill like a normal skier, I tore straight down, mind frozen on the snow in front of me, knees bent, skis launching me over the patchwork of moguls on the run and landing me with a thwump on the other side again and again. I wasn't skiing; I was falling downhill on top of skis. As I reached the bottom, our instructor was laughing. Shaking his head he commented, "Well, that was… exciting. But, I wouldn't call it skiing."

Then he said what every coach eventually says in some way or another about improving one's game, "You need to focus. What you look at and pay attention to is where the rest of your body will take you."

I had begun the run with the vague intention of skiing down the mountain. Once I began plunging downhill, I continued my descent, my brain solely absorbed with survival and the need to quickly reach the bottom and put a stop to my sense of impending disaster. Only able to focus on the mogul right in front of me, every new one I encountered as I tore downhill seemed a fresh surprise.

Although this is mostly a story about my less-than-stellar athletic abilities, it paints a picture about the need to address our larger intentions as a country. Like athletes, we need to focus our attention. Without positive visions and purposeful plans for where we are headed as a nation, our reflexes will take us in directions we don't necessarily want to go. Our instinctual minds, especially in a crisis, take over and act in survival mode, shooting us along, every new obstacle a fresh surprise.

What we spend time watching influences the course of our lives and our nation. Because of search-engine algorithms, what we choose to look at on our devices determines what additional information we're offered. We're not all being given the same data. We're not watching the same events. We're not being offered the same facts. We're not even able to begin assessing "reality" together. In an age when technology can make information instantly available, we're not only getting it from diverse sources but from altogether different and contradictory ones. Division is conceived the moment something happens. Our vision is being divided.

When our sons Andrew and Ryan were in the throes of finals their senior year at Chapman University, they made a short comedy, scraping together a $3,000 budget and using a volunteer labor force comprised of our son Braden, fellow students and friends. They found gifted actors already working in the industry who were willing to give their input on the characters they played and contributed their acting talents without pay.

In our guys' comedic film, *The Substitute*, a success-driven, white salesman is suddenly confronted by an easy-going black reflection of himself in the mirror. He goes from being egocentric, arrogant, rude and selfish to enjoying his life, wanting friendship and being able to see the world around him in fresh ways.

It's possible for stories to awaken simple desires for what truly makes us stronger, things like camaraderie and mutual success. Our storytelling is shaping our culture's values and emphasizing priorities; unfortunately not always the ones we want or need. The marketing industry knows that what occupies both our focused and subconscious attention greatly influences our values and directs our reflexive, impulsive purchasing. Much of our other media is doing the same, shaping our attitudes and behavior for the spontaneous actions we take every day.

What we do with our time, even in the privacy of our own devices, is influencing our strength and prowess as a democracy. We need to believe there is a bigger picture and both create and look for the content that will help us find a better focus. What we focus on will be where we go.

Fresh Thinking

Kuk stood with the five kids clustered around him, looking out the window of Lauri's family room in the San Gabriel foothills. With a view over downtown LA and out to the coastline, with its band of ocean reflecting sunlight, a light swirl of snow began to fall on our hilltop, making the scene magical and surreal. Kuk began to sing an impromptu "Hallelujah" and we all joined in.

Part of each homeschool week one year was spent at our friends' home, the Smiths, in their upstairs family room, with Kuk encouraging the kids to do what he was doing during those years, dream big about their futures. We would stand facing the sweeping views over Los Angeles, eyes open, praying creative prayers over our city and each other. Later, when Kuk moved with his family to Atlanta to produce music, the boys were naturally encouraged about their own futures as they saw Kuk's dreams taking shape.

The years of homeschooling worked changes in our identity as a family. Our circle of friends included a wide variety of people and professions—scientists, musicians, professors, law enforcement officers, designers, accountants, actors, auto mechanics, special event coordinators, teachers, salesmen, producers, real estate agents, chefs—and our rhythms adjusted to fit what worked best in our community and what was going on day-to-day.

If we went to see friends at a gig or nighttime performance, we wouldn't start school the next day until after we slept in, exercised and were ready to concentrate on studies. If a friend had a large design project and needed help, we would spend the day moving furniture, installing appliances and hanging pictures. The boys learned to assist at special events, helping with cooking, sound equipment, or driving golf carts for donors at fundraisers. They were part of setting up a professional recording studio and built a solid dog enclosure for a furniture-chewing pit bull. We also had many friends who simply spent time with us. We were often with them in their homes around LA, sharing meals, hanging out and experiencing aspects of their lives that gave us a better view of their different perspectives on the world.

Ultimately, I think Graeme and I were the greatest beneficiaries of those years of homeschooling. We enlarged our circle of friends and got to know our sons in ways we wouldn't have if they were spending their days in the familiar traditions of classroom education. I learned a lot in this time of life; or better said, I unlearned. The first-born in my family, I had been an unintentional legalist, following all the rules, and a firm believer in all the organizational structures, systems, forms and requirements that validate our nation's hierarchies of success. I had mostly taken at face value the predictive power and importance of things like 4.0 GPAs, high test scores and academic awards, until my circle of friends expanded to include many who had progressed through life with different attitudes and perspectives than mine.

Many of my hardline convictions about the education system in general were fading in those years. I began to believe less in the particular methods or forms of education I was familiar with—such as sitting in rows, listening to teachers and lecturers, tests and measurements—and more in finding ways to cultivate a lifelong love of learning and a commitment to understanding the world and our place in it.

I didn't just want my sons and their friends to learn how to read, I wanted them to love books. It wasn't as important as I initially thought that they learn how to print neatly, write cursive or even create grammatically correct, three-point essays; I wanted them to love communicating with people. It wasn't good enough to simply be able to list the continents, I wanted them to love the world. Gradually, over years, which was a different timeline than I often felt comfortable with, we saw various aspects of the traditional markers of a good education fall into place. It took time for the boys to gain the skills they needed to become lifelong learners, committed to their own education and character growth.

The process of homeschooling offered me the unexpected opportunity to discover that education wasn't the same thing as *the system* called education. I was afforded a perspective from a different angle that caused me to question many things I had simply taken for granted about the systems and organizations that are considered essential to our lives. I came to the conclusion that we need to examine those systems to see if they're actually accomplishing their intended purpose for everyone. Fresh thinking is in order.

Splintered Systems

Graeme was gripping an old stud in the wall as he worked on rewiring Andrew's and Ryan's house in Nashville. He adjusted his weight, pushing hard to shove a junction box into place with his right hand when a long splinter went through his left index finger on one side and poked out on the other.

With the nonchalance of an experienced construction worker, Graeme washed it off and realized he couldn't just get back to work since the wood was old, dirty and interfered with his grip. He asked the guys if one of them would pull it out with needle-nose pliers, but there wasn't enough splinter sticking out to grab. Ryan ended up driving him to the pharmacy down the street that advertised on their window they gave shots, bandaged sprains and took out splinters. As it turned out, not splinters like that. The pharmacist did an online search for an urgent care in the area, couldn't find one listed and recommended Graeme go to a local hospital emergency room.

Ryan dropped Graeme off and he went in to ask the receptionist if this was a good place to get some help with a splinter or if she could recommend another. She told him he'd come to the right place and had him fill out paperwork with his insurance information.

Over the next two hours, Graeme received "medical care" for a splinter. A nurse took his temperature, blood pressure, and pulse and showed him to a treatment cubicle. A physician's assistant asked Graeme the reason for his visit. He held up his hand and said he'd like help pulling out the splinter. She said it would be better to make sure the entire splinter was removed by cutting it out, using lidocaine and a scalpel. Graeme wasn't convinced and suggested cutting just enough skin to get a grip and pull the splinter out. She insisted her way was better, gave him the shot, let it take effect and picked up the scalpel. Graeme looked away during the procedure and looked back as a nurse put on a Band-Aid. As he left, he stopped at reception to settle his bill and was charged $108.00. End of story.

Except that over the next days and weeks, while the scalpel incision healed quickly, Graeme's finger was still very sore to the touch. About three months after the visit to the ER, Graeme noticed a small dark spot where his finger was tender, applied some pressure on either side and out came a splinter a third of an inch long. The relief from the pain he'd had the last few months was immediate.

About a month after that, a bill came from the hospital for $1,700. The amount seemed laughable, and since the bill didn't list a treatment or breakdown of costs, we assumed it had been sent by mistake. Graeme called the hospital multiple times and was finally able to determine it was his bill for the attempted splinter removal. He asked for an itemized breakdown. A list of undecipherable hospital codes and costs came in the mail. Graeme called again and eventually found someone who would send him explanations for the codes. After receiving a list that included costly items like "triage" and "diagnosis," words that seemed nonsensical given he told them he had a splinter, Graeme was able to negotiate his bill down to $300 plus the $108 he had already paid. He sent a letter to the hospital with the payment, stating it was still completely out of line to charge $408 to *not* remove a splinter.

Months after we thought the bill was finally settled, an additional bill arrived for $565, the cost of the physician assistant who did not remove the splinter. Graeme called repeatedly to inform the physician's group they had not actually removed the splinter and he wouldn't pay the additional $565. The bill continued to come each month and was eventually sent on to a collection agency.

After hours of work on Graeme's part that we obviously couldn't bill *them* for, the physician's group finally relented and notified the collection agency they "forgave" his debt. We were grateful we were forgiven, but concerned for all those who were encountering the same treatment or worse. We ultimately paid $408 of the total $2,373 that we were billed for *not* removing a splinter.

Over the years we've been thankful for the many doctors, nurses and other medical staff who have served our family well. Yet, as so many people have discovered the hard way, a medical system that operates without intelligence, integrity and compassion doesn't serve, it takes.

Simply because systems and organizations carry a name does not mean they fulfill a need. There is an obvious distinction between actual medical *care* and the medical system. There is a difference between educated children and the education system. The political system does not always provide wise leadership or the legal system, justice. Our systems for response and recovery are not accomplishing all we need them to. We need to address these as a nation.

We as individuals need to pay attention and recognize when the systems and organizations we work within are not providing the services or results they are intended to perform. We need to see it as a part of our job to change that. We're each needed to improve the functionality of our systems with the way we live our own daily lives. Simply put, we need to take responsibility for our own integrity and the soundness of our work.

Strength of character applied in each person's sphere of influence weaves itself into the systems and organizations that underpin every sector of life, every aspect of culture and the infrastructure that enables us to withstand the increased pressure of crises and disasters. We're meant to contribute our unique insight and effort to reshape the systems intended to serve us so they fulfill the purposes and provide the resources we all rely on.

Communal
Blindness

Graeme and I were arguing—not the first time, not the last. We both remember where we were on the Yolo causeway that summer in 1985 when we came to an important point of agreement we still hold today. Graeme was working for the Sacramento Municipal Utility District (SMUD) on what was at the time the world's largest photovoltaic solar project. He preferred the work he did on the renewable energy projects SMUD had: hydroelectric, geothermal and this new solar effort. But, Graeme was also required to have his nuclear power plant training up to date. Our disagreement involved a recent series of intense quality assurance classes he had attended.

Graeme had been relating how many fail-safes there were in the systems at Rancho Seco Nuclear Generating Station (the Ranch) and how he was convinced that good engineering was the most critical component of operational safety. Graeme's perspective was that if sound science was being implemented, disasters at nuclear power plants would be avoided. As a new mom and a graduate student in psychology, my life experiences were convincing me that things get messy whenever people are involved. I hotly maintained that the human actors were the most important element in any system or organization. Graeme, reasoning as an engineer, described the technologies and procedures used to ensure that reactors were always operating within certain limits and how it was not possible for people to interfere with these thorough systems.

I began to suggest a scenario close to home. A new father, sleep deprived, cranky and bleary-eyed, misreads an indicator. Seeing the humor, Graeme added details to my hypothetical story, beginning to recognize the gaps in the system when it came to completely unpredictable human behavior. By the end of our conversation that day, we were both settled in our conviction that people are a huge risk factor that cannot be completely mitigated by technology and quality assurance procedures.

The day after Christmas at the end of that year, an accident took place in the nuclear reactor vessel at the Ranch, providing an illustration that furthered our understanding of risk. A power outage in the control room, coupled with operator errors, allowed the steel vessel to cool faster than the limits designed to prevent cracking in the vessel. With alarms sounding and emergency efforts of the staff not working, one operator collapsed from stress as the team fought to stop a reactor meltdown.

Although the event didn't continue long enough for the vessel to fracture, radioactive steam was released and two employees were exposed to a level of radiation considered "safe." One of the more disconcerting aspects of this near disaster was the discovery that there had been similar difficulties at other facilities designed by the same company that built Rancho Seco. But, instead of using this information, the specific mitigation safeguards that could have prevented this accident had not been implemented at the Ranch. People with authority made decisions based on something other than scientifically motivated best practice and the welfare of the people who would be impacted.

There are many, many ways that human behavior intertwines with the concept of disaster. In this case, the connection is obvious with human-designed and operated technology. Yet, the same is true with natural hazards. Peoples' choices are often the ties that bind scientifically understood, physical phenomena to the tragedies of disaster. The highest good for the people involved is not always the highest priority.

Earthquakes destroy buildings that are not built to withstand shaking, floods inundate unprotected subways and below-grade utilities, wildfires burn and destroy the homes casually built on the urban-wild land interface and tsunamis and storm surges take out entire communities constructed in inundation zones. We put everything at risk when a predictable natural hazard is not accounted for or when an event exceeds the standards we as a society have established for the infrastructure we rely on.

Not only is new development often built in seeming defiance of the risk of predictable natural hazards, in addition, throughout the United States, the infrastructure we need to survive is aging. Our water lifelines are corroded, our reservoirs in need of repairs, our levees increasingly vulnerable, the electrical and communication systems overly exposed to natural and human hazards, and our roads, highways and bridges neglected and susceptible to failure.

Our design, engineering and construction capabilities have what it takes to address many of these risks, but we continue as a culture to make decisions based more on short-term considerations than on long-term stability. If we as Americans continue to make our routine and most important decisions based on qualities such as financial gain, expedience and convenience, the outcomes will reflect these less-than values.

We often behave as though these expected, naturally occurring events have caught us off-guard and are "surprisingly" tragic. Yet, many of the disasters we experience are the result of communal blindness to the choices we're making by our lack of participation in our democratic process or, worse, deliberately. Our everyday decision making is frequently based on priorities other than human good and the wellbeing of our communities.

Natural and man-made events and their devastating outcomes can have completely different storylines if we have a collective change of heart. It's simple really: the way to diminish risk and the disasters that follow is to care about the impact of our choices and educate ourselves about the fundamental requirements that sustain the life of the communities we love.

San Clemente Dam

During the summer of 2015, looking like kids going on a field trip, fifteen middle school and high school science teachers, two tour guides from the local water utility, and three of us from Disaster Scope climbed into vans in a school district parking lot in Carmel, California. Headed farther up the beautiful Carmel Valley, we were going to see for ourselves what practical applications of science were involved in the San Clemente Dam Removal and River Restoration Project.

The year before, Graeme and I had finished almost twelve months living and working in New York on the Hurricane Sandy Recovery, and we wanted a break from disasters. Recovery work can feel discouraging. The devastation has already happened and the analysis of damage and rebuilding costs can be an excruciating, bureaucratic process. As the work to recover is calculated and negotiated with federal, state, local and nonprofit stakeholders, the difficulties and negative attitudes that exist within the systems of daily operations before the crisis become even more apparent.

The recovery effort in Manhattan had been especially challenging. The added complexities of the Sandy Recovery Improvement Act of 2013 had contributed new difficulties to achieving the best outcomes, not to mention the political involvement that had simply negated so many people's work and awarded billions of dollars without justification. When we saw the opportunity to shift our focus to developing a means of growing long-term resilience, we wanted to pursue that possibility.

In 2014, California and other western states were experiencing an ongoing and severe drought. News from the Monterey Peninsula was especially full of bitter controversy regarding water issues. Community meetings were often contentious, with no sense of growing collaboration and little of the resolve that can build resilience. It's been our observation that where people are in crisis and their attention is focused on apparently insurmountable problems, anxiety, fear and conflicts increase.

Rather than seeing only the problem at hand, we believe it's important for communities to enlarge their perspective to include the bigger picture of the systems and the science underlying their lifelines; the infrastructure they require and rely on daily.

Our work in Monterey involved creating Water Education Today (WET), a unique program of classroom-ready water science lessons and teacher training based on current, local water utility projects. Through WET, we worked to interest teachers, students and their families (who were experiencing the severe restrictions and personal costs of drought) in important components of their local water system. Our curriculum expert, Becky McKinney, a dynamic high school physics educator, conducted training seminars for teachers using fun and engaging inquiry-based methods.

Our first workshop for the teachers included the fun field trip to the San Clemente Dam as it was readied for demolition, giving the teachers a real-life view of their community's water infrastructure. As we drove to the site that day, the teachers learned how various entities contributed funding and direction to the massive undertaking of removing the dam and restoring the river. Connecting classroom science to the multi-faceted aspects of business, science, engineering, technology, politics and social science involved in our essential community lifelines prepares the next generation of citizens for building resilience.

Wearing hard hats and yellow vests, we walked out on the dam and one of the dam operators described the various aspects of science used at the site: dam construction and maintenance, seismic analysis to declare the dam unfit, and the long list of engineering and environmental requirements that needed to be addressed on the project. He spoke about historic water levels and flow on the Carmel River, the design of the step pools being created for rainbow trout and the ecology of the red-legged frog habitat. Questions about agricultural runoff and the considerations involved in water quality were also discussed. Our lifelines require a vast number of contributors with expertise in many fields.

In addition to a reporter covering our trip to the dam and the work the teachers were doing to help students understand local water science, Paola Berthoin, a local artist, was painting a series of landscapes at the site. Her book, *Passion for Place,* is a unique compilation of 45 local community members—poets, writers, photographers and other artists—seeking to raise awareness about the importance of protecting the region's watershed and lifeline.

When these types of collaborations between businesses, utilities, schools, science, arts, media and government are created, we generate positive discussions and innovation that continue to move our communities toward resilient outcomes.

Key investments made in education always pay dividends. Our nation needs public and private sponsors willing to fund science, technology, engineering, art and math in the specific ways that inspire students to build resilient community life and strengthen the lifelines that make it possible. We need to respect and support our teachers and the programs that empower them to stay abreast of the ways their subject matter is relevant to the challenges our communities are experiencing so that we can continue to move forward together in finding the solutions we need.

Food for All

Linda and I (ages 6 and 8) climbed over mounds of dirt at the edge of the field toward the rows of cotton where Granddad Burden was standing talking to the farmer about his vegetable crops for the season. We were making slow progress, trying to keep most of the dirt out of our sandals, hoping he'd see us and come our way. Granddad was working the fields of Orange County for a few days, determining with the farmers what the best harvest times were for their different crops so that Prime Frozen Foods, the company he worked for in Pasadena, could predict the freezing schedule at the plant.

I remember this particular day because I was surprised to discover that bright, clean cotton balls grew on bushes from boll bracts that were hard and spikey. The cotton that would become cloth looked a lot like what was kept in a glass container on our bathroom counter, but in trying to pull a ball of it off the bush, I made my finger bleed. Being out in that field would later give me a context for history lessons about cotton and slavery.

I also remember the overwhelming sound of the bees. They were everywhere and buzzing so loudly that it seemed like a threat. I had stepped on a bee a few days before and knew how much it hurt, so I was apprehensive about the thousands of menacing creatures now buzzing around me.

Granddad looked our way and touched the rim of his cowboy hat with a grin. He wrapped up his conversation, shook hands with his colleague and came toward us. Granddad moved easily over the uneven earth the way a sailor handles the pitch of the sea. Like our dad, he was over six feet tall, with a stride that covered the distance quickly. As he bent down to pick up Linda, I told him I was afraid of the bees and he told me that although they sounded loud down where I was, they were too busy working to bother me. I tried to walk beside him unafraid, as though I believed him.

Years later, when I would join my friend Renee Guilbault at her meetings on food policy around LA, I would remember times in the fields with my grandfather. One of the many topics that came up in discussions was the need to protect pollinators like those bees in the cotton field from pesticides and other pollution that threaten their welfare and our food supply.

After years of working as a chef and a food and beverage executive, Renee established a consulting business. Often, she contributes her time and the insights she's gained to influence decisions that impact our food availability, access and utilization. I've learned a lot about this lifeline as I've hung out with her. It's a fun way to learn. We eat a lot of delicious food.

When my sisters and I were little, our summers were filled with fresh produce still warm from the fields.

Granddad would come back to town with lugs of tomatoes, flats of strawberries and boxes of beans. In those years we also had bottles of fresh milk from local dairies delivered to our back door early every morning, and the milkman would take our empties back to be sterilized and refilled for the next morning's delivery. A truck from a local bakery would drive down our street with racks of freshly baked bread, pies and pastries for sale in the afternoons. When I was a girl, there were still a lot of chicken coups in LA neighborhoods and our eggs from the grocery store came from farms close by.

Over the years, I've watched our food production move farther and farther away from us. In Southern California, most of the farms, dairies and ranches that supplied our tables have given way to housing and commercial buildings. When food isn't grown locally, the journey it takes to arrive in our grocery stores is complex and, even under the best circumstances, logistically complicated. Following any unforeseen events that impact ports, roads, bridges and gasoline our food lifelines are compromised in some way.

In Los Angeles, Renee served for a while on the mayor's Food Policy Council, which worked with other organizations to create a more just and sustainable food system. Many cities across the country have formed these organizations where people with different expertise and interests in food production, delivery and access within a community contribute their perspective and policy advice regarding local food issues.

Renee worked on a project that I found especially relevant to disaster resilience called the Los Angeles Foodshed. It's not a hut with food in it, it's the big-picture or strategic view of where food comes from and how it reaches all the people throughout a region. By addressing the weaknesses in the routine supply and distribution of food in a geographic area and those people and places that are typically underserved and vulnerable, we can better identify and address where this lifeline may fail in a crisis.

When we see to the daily needs of the poor by ensuring access to nutritious food for everyone, we actually increase all of our resilience. Understanding food distribution, looking at how our food system operates, discovering where it's fragile and working to strengthen the accessibility of healthy food within our communities is a great way to increase our disaster resilience.

Party for the Soul

It was a beautiful night in 2016 at Doheny Beach when my friend Diane and I entered the second-story restaurant to attend Party for the Soul. My friends Chris and Karyn Falson design events like this to bring people together for a night of fun and refreshment. It's something they've done around Europe, their homeland of Australia, and in many venues around Southern California. Our family had met them Valentine's Day in 1999 at a similar event they were hosting with a friend, James Langteaux, at his rooftop loft on top of the old converted Pabst Blue Ribbon Brewery. Their desire is to bring people together, creating space and atmosphere for them to hang out and form community connections and friendships.

We went out on the deck where there were appetizers and cocktails waiting to help get the party going. We plopped down on a sofa overlooking the rocky ocean breakwater and leaned back, ready to enjoy ourselves. The Rhythm Gospel and Blues band had started their first set, with Chris leading. Soon, the sounds of the music drowned out the freeway stress we'd all driven through to get there. The party had started.

The noise in the place picked up with the sounds of people having a good time as the last colors of sunset disappeared into the foggy night sky. By now, everyone was talking and laughing like old friends. Discovering that we were similar ages and had grown up in the adjacent towns of Eagle Rock and Pasadena, Dina Gilio-Whitaker and I shared those factoids new acquaintances offer about themselves, touching on our childhoods, high school experiences and travels in life since then.

As we talked, I mentioned the kind of work we do, and that Graeme had just left to help with the Louisiana Spring Flood recovery and that I would be moving to Baton Rouge shortly to join him and continue writing this book. Dina responded by telling me she had just completed co-authoring her own book, *All The Real Indians Died Off: And 20 Other Myths About Native Americans.*

I was intrigued. My childhood love of Native Americans, born through watching Roy Rogers, Dale Evans and my early memories of Disneyland came to mind, and I peppered Dina with questions. She answered with personal stories and researched information that was new to me. I began the humbling process of recognizing I didn't know what I didn't know when it came to the original population of the continent. We'd all do well to acknowledge how much we don't really understand and still need to learn about the history of the land and people.

One of the concepts Dina introduced to me that night was the influence Native Americans had on the development of the Constitution of the United States. I don't recall learning anything in history class about the Great Peacemaker or the Iroquois Confederacy. I had never heard about the long-established, peaceful cooperation between five different tribes in what is now the eastern

United States. Interestingly, this historic event was marked by a total solar eclipse in 1142 AD, centuries before the Pilgrims' arrival. Evidently, this tribal association for mutual benefit was familiar to Benjamin Franklin and the others who participated in crafting the union of the original colonies.

I ordered her book and continued to grow my awareness. I kept in touch with Dina as she and her co-author traveled around the country on their book tour. Unexpectedly, the book's release coincided with the extensive media coverage of the protests of the Dakota Access Pipeline (DAP). Reports of the blatant disregard of Native American concerns, the environment, and the water and land rights at Standing Rock, South Dakota were in the news and throughout social media. Dina's and Roxanne's book was timely and its popularity was immediate.

Because of our education and disaster experience, events like the pipeline protest get our attention. Having lived through severe droughts, with an awareness of water scarcity on a daily basis, this reality has been reinforced over and over: water is precious. It's hard to live in California and not know that water lifelines are fragile and precarious for a wide variety of reasons. Water required for the common good needs protecting. This is a truth not just in the West where water is scarce but everywhere on the planet where a multitude of factors put water security at risk.

Our work in Monterey County on water-related issues reinforced our opinion that essential water lifelines should always be given priority. In any construction, development or industrial project, concerns about water security must be thoroughly investigated and addressed.

Every single American would do well to understand the importance of clean and accessible water and our rights to this essential and threatened necessity.

As the protest in South Dakota continued, we became alarmed as we heard stories and saw images of attack dogs and water cannons being used against protestors, reminiscent of the Civil Rights Era. It was inconceivable that our country's authorities were again condoning the use of force against protestors peacefully exercising essential and fundamental rights. These events, this disregard of human dignity, along with the blocking of traditional and social media access and coverage, were alarming. Surely we are capable of finding ways forward that don't result in harming others or limiting our freedoms.

As we read the different arguments and motivations for violently pressing ahead with the pipeline, it became clear that many didn't understand the possible consequences. Some made it sound as though the project was essential infrastructure and that time was of the essence, yet few on the side of the oil industry seemed to recognize or address the primary importance of water over the other considerations involved.

I understood from Dina, who interviewed protest leaders in South Dakota about their meetings with the DAP representatives, that the tribe's concerns about water pollution and the desecration of their sacred lands had never really been heard or considered. We as a nation were repeating our past offenses with violent action taken against sovereign tribal nations. If we're going to put our trust in democracy, then we must make sure that all voices are heard and not disregarded to our detriment. We must incorporate the whole truth in the decisions we make. The people protesting at Standing Rock weren't interfering with essential infrastructure development, as some claimed, they were asserting that financial interests were overriding wise stewardship of our most essential resource: water. We must be discerning. Our lives depend on it.

Heavy Burden or
Oracle of Wisdom

"We've just received a report that the space shuttle, Challenger, exploded this morning 73 seconds after its launch at Cape Canaveral, Florida." I was listening to the radio on my way to a doctor's appointment when I heard the news.

Many of those I grew up with had our identities intertwined with NASA's space program. It wasn't just that our parents worked at Caltech and Jet Propulsion Laboratory. Caltech was an extension of our homes. We ate at facilities on campus, enjoyed different education programs, and we spent our summers at the pool the way other kids hang out at the city plunge or country club. Our swimming classes were often taught by aspiring rocket scientists. When you are 11, having a nerdy but handsome diving instructor coach you by talking about vectors and "optimum angles of entry for minimal disruption at impact," when all you want to do is avoid another face-planting gut-smacker off the three-meter board while trying to nail a backflip, NASA makes something of a permanent imprint.

The rhythms of our family schedules followed the rhythms of the space program. My friends and I were excited when our parents got to be at Cape Canaveral for a launch as spacecraft left to explore places like Mars, Venus and Mercury. We celebrated when projects succeeded and shared the disappointment when projects foundered.

In January of 1986 when NASA's Challenger launched, many students were watching on school televisions because the first teacher in space, Christa McAuliffe, was onboard. It wasn't just those of us with long connection to the space program who were shocked watching news of the space shuttle explosion just moments into flight. The loss was felt in homes around the country where families, interested in Challenger's mission as an educational milestone, had a connection to Christa.

In the days following, the loss seemed even more tragic as information about the cause of the explosion became clear: small and vital parts of the solid rockets, the O-rings, had been known to fail at the cold temperatures that existed the morning of the launch. It was human error that caused the catastrophe.

Engineers at the company that manufactured the O-rings knew the design limitations and had warned NASA the solid rockets would fail given the expected cold weather. In fact, the night before, the company's representative had refused to sign the launch recommendation. Still, the launch went ahead and the preventable disaster and loss of life took place, devastating family members and all those who watched it. Children watching around the country were robbed of their innocence.

One of the engineers who predicted the mission would fail in cold weather and had attempted to stop the launch spoke in an interview on the thirtieth anniversary of the disaster. Although he had acted professionally and given his supervisors all they needed to make an informed decision, he continued to feel personally responsible for not having done more to abort the mission. He spoke of carrying this heavy *emotional burden* of personal responsibility for thirty years.

Because I think names have significance, when I hear my family name, Burden, being used to describe a heavy load or an emotional weight, I also think about the lesser-known meaning, "Oracle: an authoritative or wise expression or answer." I've noticed over the years that when something is described as a heavy burden, there is also the potential for an oracle of wisdom or an insight to come through the experience.

It's ironic that in the cases of preventable disaster, the power to make decisions is often outside the authority of those who have the most pertinent facts. The final decisions are often made by those who focus less on the human investment and exercise more concern about the money, position or reputation that's at stake. There are many throughout our culture who feel the frustration of being unheard and prevented from seeing the good their work is intended to accomplish. We need to place a higher value and greater expectations on our leaders to listen to and include the relevant expertise and research in their decision making, especially when it comes to factors that contribute to disaster.

DNA

Our family stories have a hand in shaping who we are. In America, many of us have ancestry that combines the blood of people who were, at one time or another, hostile to each other over the centuries. It has struck me how the lineage I rattle off when asked—Scottish, Irish, Danish, Dutch, Welsh, English, Norwegian, French, and Spanish—contains ethnic groups who were at war with one another at different times in history. The English battled the Scots, the Vikings raided the British Isles, and folks on the Continent fought and killed each other with abandon. Ultimately, if we go back far enough, we are all the product of stories of love and hate that defy the national and ethnic boundaries we maintain today. This is especially true for Americans.

Recently, two of my friends had genetic testing done, one for medical reasons and the other on a lark. They were both surprised by what their DNA told them. A friend from Mexico discovered her blood work included markers from Ashkenazic and Sephardic Jews from France and Spain. Some of her longstanding questions about her grandmother's unusual behaviors every Friday night—of drawing the curtains, lighting candles for dinner and leaving certain foods off the menu at different times of year were answered. Another friend who expected her blood work to indicate that she was half Armenian, a quarter Mexican and a quarter European found she had a different heritage than the one her maternal, Armenian grandparents were emphatically convinced solely defined them. She was less than half Armenian. It's best we keep open hearts of compassion, recognizing that our original ethnic description is the simplest: we are all part of the *human* race.

Whether we are certain of our bloodline or not, we have in us the forgotten stories of generations: of plenty and lack, the loving and the unfaithful, conquerors and their conquered, abuser and abused. We get to choose with our thoughts, words and behavior what aspects will ultimately define us and tell in the final determination of our identity. We can each choose to be the best and noblest of our heritage and contribute that to the whole of who we are as a people.

Heritage

My grandmother Burden once told me about how the girls and young women from her church in their farming community in Kansas helped to raise funds one Sunday by preparing picnic basket lunches to be auctioned off to the highest bidder. She said Granddad had "bid special" on her basket and "that was that." There's very little I know about their lives. My grandparents were disinclined to talk much about their parents or the harsh poverty of their childhoods. Only rarely did they mention what they knew of their mostly forgotten immigrant and native heritage of English, Irish, and Cherokee.

The Midwest was experiencing a disaster known as the Dust Bowl in the 1930s, and not long after they were married my grandparents left their farming town in the state of Kansas for "the big city" of Kansas City, Missouri. Barely able to get by and with a third baby on the way, Granddad answered an ad in the local paper looking for men with gas money to transport a car from Kansas to the West. Traveling with five strangers who also wanted an inexpensive way to get across the country, he arrived in Stockton, California and moved into a chicken coup with "Uncle Ira the Communist."

My grandfather worked at what he could find in local fields, pulling weeds from irrigation ditches, knocking trees with wooden bats to harvest walnuts, and digging countless postholes for fencing. In Kansas City, in a small walk-up apartment with shared kitchen and bathroom facilities, my grandmother worked to make ends meet, taking in laundry and ironing as she cared for her two young sons.

Before long Granddad had saved enough for train tickets for the family to join him and Uncle Ira in California. Dad tells stories about sleeping head to toe on cots and beds in the converted chicken coup, of the treat it was to get chips of ice off the block needed to keep the icebox cool and of working together at whatever would contribute to the family's survival.

After moving on again to Los Angeles in search of work, Granddad first washed dishes at a Jewish hospital and then found a job at a frozen vegetable processing plant in Pasadena. Soon the family was able to join him there. Eventually he became a field supervisor, overseeing the timing of harvests, traveling to farms throughout Southern California. I think the respect of the men he worked for meant even more to him than his accomplishment of finally being able to buy a home.

Granddad was a poor man with a seventh-grade education, loyal to his boss and company. When he was first working on the plant floor he came home and told my dad he'd seen a worker slip a box of vegetables under his shirt. He had been reluctant to report him and so had walked over to the man and quietly said, "I don't think you meant to do that," took the box and told him to get back to work. Later when the shift ended, Granddad paid for the box and sent it home with him.

I recall him teaching me this same compassion one day at the grocery store in the mid-1960s when the manager and another customer were complaining about immigrant farmworkers, the boycotts and lack of grapes. My grandfather, usually quiet, spoke up, "Those people work hard and I'm thinking they're as entitled to minimum wage as anybody." His quiet empathy for others, born of his own hard experiences, became a family value.

My mom is of Danish descent on her mom's side, and as far as she knows, a mix of Irish, Scots, Dutch and Welsh on her dad's. Her mother used to say, "You're half Danish and half alley cat." Her parents met at Trinity Baptist church in Long Beach where my grandfather was visiting one Sunday with his mother. He spotted my grandmother in the choir, pointed to her and said, "See there, Mother, that's the woman I'm going to marry." Granddad had an expansive personality. My mom remembers him dressing in boxing shorts without a shirt when he mowed the lawn, posing for his family and neighbors, fists raised, arms flexed to show off his physique, laughingly calling their attention to how much he looked like Rocky Graziano, the middle-weight boxing champion of the world in 1947.

During the Great Depression and World War II, my mom's dad worked in the office at the Crown City Dairy. Mom remembers they often set an extra plate at the dinner table for different men who had come into the dairy looking for work. Granddad may have had to turn them down for a job, but he did so with the promise of an evening meal and a bed for the night. The hospitality he showed to strangers was something my mother inherited and has passed down to my sisters and me.

As individuals, we all inherit more than just property, finances or genetic material. We inherit character, ethics and perspectives. Sometimes we consciously adopt those things we admire. At other times we try to avoid the mistakes we have witnessed or the pain we've experienced. Many of us incorporate new ways of thinking. Yet, some never grow as human beings and routinely make self-serving decisions. When we recognize that our beliefs about what is most important are fashioned to some extent by our past experiences, we're able to see with more clarity and can wisely build for the future.

India's Value Education

I greeted our family friend Dr. George Samuel as I entered the house, carrying a box of books into the hall. He was visiting from India and staying with his boyhood friend Sam in Sierra Madre, a mountainside neighborhood near us. Sam and his wife, Leela, worked with University of Southern California students and they were helping George collect donated books for the seminary library being built in their hometown in India. I was delivering what our family and friends had been able to gather for the effort.

Our two families had become friends in the 1970s when George was doing his residency in nuclear medicine at Harbor-UCLA Medical Center. Over the years, like so many other friends, he had shared meals around our table and given us a view of his country and our world through his eyes. Forty years later, it's more often his daughter, Anne and his grandson Nikhil, who come for visits and hang out with Graeme and me, inspiring us with a larger perspective on the issues the world is facing.

As we sat and talked that day at Sam's house, George told me about the seminars he was giving in schools and colleges throughout India and in the Middle East. He was urging the implementation of value-based education, the concept of teaching all subject matter with the intention of accomplishing more than simply the impartation of information. Specifically, he explained his desire to see science, technological advancement, business and industry in India and other countries bring about widespread benefit and wellbeing for people and their communities. Too often, in any country, economic development does not ensure community development. It takes inspiration, deliberate planning and consistent, long-term attention to translate the acquisition of personal or corporate wealth into beneficial actions that move society forward and increase the quality of life for all people, their communities and the environment.

There are many leaders within India who are convinced that the rote acquisition of subject matter is not an adequate education for promoting the overall prosperity of India and her people. George pointed out the hopeful nature of India's consensus, that even with their diversity of religious beliefs and cultures, many values such as love, peace, honesty, self-control, joy, kindness and respect are still shared in common. His contention is that the same will work anywhere.

The news is full of the epic failures of financial institutions, government, and industry. All of us in America have clearly seen how the character of individuals profoundly impacts our society's holistic success. Exploring together ways to teach the Golden Rule and to prize good character will be transformational for our communities and world.

Just as I experienced as a child growing up in school, George sees school as a potent environment to inspire the next generation. He says the educational system is a natural place to encourage shared values for business, industry and government. Academic and business achievements are not enough in and of themselves to elevate a society. Ultimately, it is the ethical behavior of individuals within the systems and organizations they control that will be most telling in India's and any country's future. George teaches a principle taken from Greek philosophy: character is destiny.

If It's Not Relational, It's Not Real

It was Thanksgiving and we had a long table set up in the living room for 18 family and friends. We had finished the feast and were feeling satisfied and relaxed as we sat with our last bites of dessert and cups of coffee, different ones taking turns telling stories that had all of us laughing.

Jason, a friend in the music industry, caught the table's attention as he opened with, "I was shaving my head in the hotel room." He continued, "I had the TV on and I couldn't believe all the politicians and different people who were kissing the Pope's ring." Scheduled to accompany his boss, Kelly Clarkson, later that day as she sang *Ave Maria* for the pope, he wondered if everybody kneeling and kissing the pope's ring were Catholic. Jason said out loud in the empty hotel room, "Geez, I would never do that!"

Then Jason began describing how his trip from the hotel to the performance venue was more stressful than usual. Although the roads were cleared of traffic, their vehicle was stopped repeatedly at police barricades along the way and the driver was required to show their passes. During the slow ride across town, Jason realized he shouldn't have had that second coffee and should have used the bathroom before he got in the car. He told us about the huge crowds of people they drove by and how, once he was out of the car and being directed on foot, there were concentric circles of security as they got closer to the pope: first the police, then secret service agents with their black suits and earpieces, and finally an inner circle of Swiss Guard. His heart was racing as he became more and more nervous that none of these men smiled or seemed to approve of him in general with his shaved head, eyebrow ring and tattoos. When he joked with one of the men about how extreme the security seemed, he was told solemnly there were snipers positioned ready to take down anyone who made a false move. Jason had enough time waiting in the wings to wonder what exactly constituted "a false move." He wondered if he could unwittingly make one.

By the time Jason was playing the grand piano onstage, he moved instinctually through the motions with confidence, trying to stay present enough to both perform well and form a clear memory of this epic moment. He came to the end of the performance, rose with relief and the intention to get off stage and find a bathroom as quickly as possible, only to find his path to the stairs was blocked by a big, silent Swiss guardsman, unwilling to let him pass. Jason was firmly directed back toward the throne where the pope was sitting. Vaguely, Jason wondered if this was a false move. Was he about to be shot? Trying to process, he found himself alone and directly in front of the pope. Jason described how surreal the moment felt, like sleepwalking, moving toward the pope in slow motion, snipers trained on him, kneeling... and kissing the pope's ring. We roared with laughter.

Later that Thanksgiving, we all watched the video online. Jason had looked professional and composed on stage. He stood, was redirected by a Swiss guard, walked across the platform, bent over quickly, kissed the ring and walked off stage. Most people viewing the video would assume they knew something about Jason and his loyalties. But, we all knew better. In minutes Jason had gone from being the guy proclaiming in his hotel room, "I would *never* kiss the pope's ring," to being the guy who just did.

We often say that actions speak louder than words. Sometimes they don't. We've been told that a picture's worth a thousand words. But sometimes, like Jason, mired in our humanity, we say and do things in a moment for reasons that are unfathomable even to ourselves. We need to truly listen to each other, even when we think we already have enough information to judge. We need to stop buying into the celebrity and social media culture that manufactures the image of a character and presents it as though it's reality, an authentic person. Getting to know each other as we sit around a table, eating, laughing and sharing our stories is the way for us to grow our understanding of each other. If it's not relational, it's not real.

Massai Cowboys

In 2011, my parents invited us over for lunch when they had two Massai from Tanzania staying with them for a few weeks. When James and Solomon had arrived on this first trip away from eastern Africa, they had stood at my parents' kitchen sink, watching with an evident sense of the surreal as water gushed from the spout. They took turns lifting and lowering the handle, unaccustomed to the convenience and abundance of water. As we sat eating together, a small fountain splashing on the patio, they described the severe scarcity of water at home and told us a story of a drought in which three-quarters of their cattle had perished.

We talked about the different cattle-ranching practices they had observed on their trip through central California, the abundance of water obviously available, and the methods of raising cattle in Tanzania compared to those in the United States. Ironically, this happened to be the year one of the worst droughts in California's history began. The evident abundance of water they witnessed was more a product of our American delusion of the unlimited availability of natural resources than the reality of those resources. It would have behooved the California ranchers to ask the Tanzanians for their ideas on cattle ranching as well. Clean and abundant water is a reality most of us take for granted.

James and Solomon had brought intricately beaded gifts from home and gave my dad a beautiful Massai warrior's club for his 80th birthday. They told him it was to be held in the middle when he was speaking to the family as an elder. With a twinkle in their eyes, they told all of us to pay attention to how he held the club because holding it by the end meant Dad was ready to enforce his authority with a fight.

There were many memorable times on their month-long visit. Once they were out shopping in their colorful Massai robes and a girl of about 8 pulled her father across the parking lot toward James and Solomon, obviously wanting to meet them. When she asked if they were Massai, they were particularly pleased to be recognized by an American child so far from home based solely on their appearance. They happily answered her questions and for a while, the small group enjoyed a lively conversation. She related what she knew from school about the Massai. James told her about the school where he teaches and Solomon told her about the lion he had killed when he was a boy, protecting his family's cattle.

On another occasion during their visit, my parents' friends from Taipei suggested they all have dinner together at one of their favorite restaurants. There was a lot of shared laughter as the Africans enjoyed both their first "all you can eat" buffet and their first Chinese food. Our family has found multi-cultural experiences like these to be rich and especially life-giving. My parents always say they are the ones who have benefitted from showing hospitality to strangers, a thought repeated throughout the

Bible. In one place the admonition comes with a supernatural enticement. Opening one's heart to strangers opens the possibility of receiving a messenger from God. We have found this to be true over and over.

The attitude of hostility some Americans display toward those from "outside" is profoundly unproductive and closed-minded. For thousands of years, those who have traveled and seen the world have brought back to their homes new insight, inventions, flavors and increased understanding from other countries. The same motivation to travel, see new things and discover what we didn't know before we left gives us reason to welcome and embrace people from other cultures moving through the space we find familiar and call home. Opening our hearts, our minds and our lives to learn from the people outside our small realms within the US will make us wiser and better able to find the keys needed to lead the world toward true success and real peace.

Uganda, CA

We were sitting at dinner with our sons Ryan and Braden one night in 2013, when Braden said with a grin, "Well, Ryan and I had some fun on a visit to Uganda today." Graeme and I had no idea what he was talking about; as far as we knew, the guys had just driven a few hours south for some work.

Ryan was in LA, visiting from Nashville to get extra footage for a music video he was directing. The two had left Pasadena early in the morning to drive to San Diego and had wrapped up in time to make it home for dinner.

It turned out the guys had been filming Bob Goff, the Honorary Consul of the Republic of Uganda and author of *Love Does*. In one of those strange facts of diplomatic relations between countries, his office in Southern California is officially part of the nation of Uganda. Memories of my childhood friends from Uganda, sharing stories and meals together, came drifting back as the guys told us about their film shoot and the humanitarian legal work that resulted in Bob's appointment as the Ugandan Consul.

This is just another fitting metaphor for the way our lives on the globe are connected. Service on the African continent *literally* resulted in a piece of it taking up residence on the North American continent.

Our interconnections are myriad and our dependencies intertwined. The answers to the global challenges we face are not necessarily resident in the geography where the problems exist. We require the wisdom, nuances and inspiration contained within the cultures of the world to create the visions we need to make our planet a place where we and future generations can thrive.

Chinatown

The sky was unusually blue and the gardens, still wet from the early morning watering, reflected the sunlight in ways that made the Huntington Gardens seem like the plein-air paintings housed in the various galleries on the expansive grounds. The day felt refreshing and the lecture we heard on the patio of the mansion was intriguing. When we attended the opening of an exhibit about a piece of Los Angeles history at the Huntington Library, Graeme and I encountered an excellent example of how a small group of marginalized Americans exercised the vision and clarified focus required for rebuilding a community.

With little warning and no say in the matter, the people of LA's original Chinatown had their homes and businesses demolished to make way for the building of the Union Station railroad facilities in the 1930s. The pervasive societal and legal opposition to the presence of "Orientals" in California was substantial, as evidenced by many things but especially the Chinatown massacre in 1871 and the federal Chinese Exclusion Act of 1882.

Through the Huntington's film footage, architectural drawings and legal documents, we recognized the exceptional and noteworthy resilience of the men and women who founded the New Chinatown. Even more interesting was the evidence throughout the exhibit of familial love and the acceptance of their new culture, with imagery from typical American home movie scenes of a child's birthday party, a family's traditional celebration around a Christmas tree and a boy enamored with his cowboy hat, boots and toy pistols as he played in his backyard.

In key ways, this moment in LA's history replicated the destruction that communities experience during disasters and the choices they face during recovery. Y.C. Hong, one of the first American attorneys of Chinese descent in California, and other leaders from the demolished Chinatown neighborhood resolved to create a vision for a stronger community. Using their various skills—artistic, business, real estate, legal, architectural—they worked together after the devastation of losing their homes and businesses to buy property and design and construct architecturally significant buildings and plazas. These not only became homes and businesses for their families but also landmarks and tourist destinations for the rest of us.

The outcome of their resilience and resolve to rise stronger is something the larger community of Los Angeles and her visitors have enjoyed throughout the years since. The businesses, restaurants and outdoor spaces created by a group of people determined to see their way through to a positive outcome and better future strengthened all of us. We can learn from these Chinese Americans that it is possible for the problems we face to actually unite and motivate us toward achieving new goals that benefit everybody.

Grandpa Great

On mornings when I'm home in California, I like to ride my bike through the neighborhood. Part of my route takes me through the alley behind the little rental cottage where my great-grandfather Tom Willadsen lived at the end of his life. I remember him as a very old man, much older than my grandparents, sitting in an upholstered rocking chair in the tiny living room, often holding a large magnifying glass in gnarled hands to read the Bible that always lay open on the table. It's a comforting picture: this family elder, sitting in contemplative silence. For years I assumed that the bronze-cast praying hands that we had on a side table in the living room were his, the way the small bronze-cast baby shoe on the bookshelf was my grandmother's.

My memories of him are fuzzy. My mother would send us girls out to play while she and "Grandpa Great" would talk. So I have more vivid recollections of the alley behind his cottage and the playtimes there with my sisters than I do of Grandpa. He passed away at 92 when I was only 7.

My mother tells a story about Grandpa Great, one of her more meaningful memories of her mother's father.

She remembers being a little girl of about six, visiting their house in Altadena in the 1930s, when her grandfather came in from trimming the rose bushes along the fence. Evidently, he and a neighbor walking by had struck up a conversation and Grandpa wanted to share with the rest of the family what he found funny.

"Do you know what that old man was worried about? He was going on about how America is going to become such a melting pot that in another 500 years or so the whole country will have brown skin. Imagine! Imagine an old man being concerned about what color skin folks are going to have. I told him if that was all he had to worry himself about, he should thank the good Lord."

When I ride my bike down Grandpa Great's alley, past people taking out the trash or working in the garages, I often feel nostalgic for the kind of family love that dies with each generation's passing. He's been gone more than fifty years and the neighbors have obviously changed over time, but I like to imagine that the people I see know my grandfather as their neighbor. A simple time warp.

My great-grandfather emigrated from Denmark with his family in 1881 when he was 7. I don't know, but he might have had his own prejudices about people different from him. Yet, I like to think that he'd feel a sense of connection with these modern neighbors who have mostly emigrated from various countries in the Middle East. I imagine all of them easily recognizing that they have a lot in common. I could see them happily swapping stories on their front steps.

In his day, the cottages were filled with other Scandinavian immigrants who owned or worked in the shops and businesses nearby. Now those same homes and shops are mostly inhabited by Armenian immigrants. I imagine them comparing coffee styles and discussing the similarities and differences between a cheese Danish and a cheese boureg, emphasizing the things they have in common and arguing, the way friends do, about the relative merits of their country's cuisine. They would share their favorite dishes on their different holidays and come to appreciate the variety.

Our nation of immigrants doesn't need to live divided by the countries we've come from. Other than the Native Americans who have been our reluctant hosts, we've all come from somewhere else. As we share our lives, our food and our cultures with each other, we are all better off. Finding connection and commonality in the simple fact of our different backgrounds can actually give us a mutual love of country, strengthen our resilience and enlarge our problem-solving capabilities.

The Best Ham

The gym I ride my bike to when we're home is a lot like the old television show *Cheers,* where the regulars who enter are greeted by folks calling out their name in welcome. I'm grateful for this community of unusually diverse women, ranging in age from 19 to 92, and a beautiful variety of shapes and sizes. Some arrive by foot, others by bike, car and bus. A few need canes to walk any distance. One walks from home with her guide dog. Some have always exercised; others have just begun. If a child were using crayons to draw us, she would need a box full of colors just to capture the flesh tones.

Our ethnicities are different and our cultures are diverse. We come from different states and parts of the world and taken as a whole, we contain a vast amount of wisdom and life experience. My friend Laura has said that between us all we have the know-how and resources to survive any emergency. She jokes, saying that it's likely going to be the crazies among us who save the day if a disaster strikes. It'll be the ones with the odd hobbies that translate into the needed emergency expertise. She's quick with examples: the hunter with cases of homemade venison jerky, the hoarder with cases of candles in her basement, or the taxidermist who also knows how to set a leg and stitch a wound.

I get exercise at other gyms around the country on my travels, often using my home membership at other locations. I've got to say that the concentrated female wisdom available where women work out is more valuable than the exercise. I've heard young moms recovering from childbirth get well-practiced advice from experienced mothers and grandmothers, found out about flash mobs from a young woman much cooler than me, learned from widows how they're learning to thrive now that they're on their own, and been given an old family recipe for a glazed ham. I was welcomed like a sister by Carlene, the owner in Houston's gym, who grew up in my California hometown's namesake, Pasadena, Texas. I got the inside scoop on the best barbecue, Thai and Indian restaurants from Sudha, the owner in Austin. Women share what they know. My experience confirms the research that shows we're more collaborative than men.

It was at my neighborhood gym, not an Emergency Operation Center or Joint Field Office, where I learned the important role that amateur radio can play in disaster when other communication is compromised. Laura, who works at a ham radio outlet with her husband, Mike, was so enthusiastic about ham radio that Graeme and I investigated how it's used in disaster. As a result, we took classes and passed a test to be ham operators. Subsequently, the ham radio folks at Caltech included us in their lunchtime meetings, patiently trying to help us get the hang of bandwidths and repeaters. While we haven't continued to participate, we're still connected to the community of people who are expert and practiced in amateur radio, one of the best forms of communication on the planet.

We also learned that since there are no uniform building codes applicable to the construction of cell phone towers, the cell networks we are overly dependent on are profoundly susceptible to a variety of natural hazards. Ham radio is vital for maintaining communications in the event of a disaster, an important component of any resilient community. In fact, in 2014, FEMA and the American Radio Relay League signed a Memorandum of Agreement enhancing cooperation between the two organizations in this area.

As our communication systems become more dependent on cell technology and internet connectivity, it's important that our laws, regulations and codes continue to be updated in ways that maintain and improve our resilience. Also, it's essential that we make sure that amateur radio continues to thrive, perhaps by including it within science curriculum in the schools. We need to ensure we continue to have an active network of volunteer radio operators throughout the country ready to assist when disasters occur. But, when all is said and done, the most reliable communication network we can build is the one we share with each other when we connect face to face and find the places where "everybody knows your name."

Pirates and Possibilities

There were armed pirates in San Pedro Harbor, California, in January 2015. Twenty-four skilled men armed with rifles, handguns, knives and grenades were focused and intent on using a ship for an impressive act of terrorism. They had boarded the moored 454-foot merchant vessel and taken 11 of its crew hostage. They were thought to be spread out, some guarding the hostages in an unknown location in the ship and others in the engine room, pilot house, cargo hold and main deck. Fortunately, a team of Navy Seals was nearby when a crew member who had managed to escape made the 911 call. Shortly, the Seals had the ship in sight and were preparing to board. Knowing there were only minutes to both rescue the hostages and stop potential devastation, the team quickly assessed their options for boarding, since there were no gangplanks. Two of their number began climbing the anchor lines at bow and stern.

Braden, our youngest son, was one of the pirates that day and he was armed with replica guns, smoke and flash grenades, and a rubber knife. As you've probably guessed, the scenario was a training exercise for Navy Seals who needed to hone their expertise in hostage situations. When the day was over, a couple of the Seals that Braden had managed to "take down" asked him what branch of the service he had served in. He grinned and said, "I'm not military. I just like to play."

Since this discussion involves guns, an especially volatile and painful topic, let me share a bit about where I'm coming from.

I don't "believe" in guns. By that, I mean that I don't believe that the best way to handle disputes is with weaponry or any kind of hostile behavior. It's never our best recourse. I am a mother who understands the sacrifice it takes to grow a human. Mothers have invested a powerful amount of effort into making people. We deserve to have our opinions weighted with the relevance of our completely singular abilities and contributions. We are the ones with the most human and social capital, blood, sweat and tears invested in human beings. And historically, we have had our voices valued least.

When my boys were little, I had a "no toy guns" policy. My reasoning was that I wanted my sons to spend their time doing the hard work of learning how to be creators. Destroying something is easy. Any toddler or fool can do that.

Creating requires cultivation, inspiration and skill. So, from the time the boys were little, they had a wide variety of toys for designing, fashioning and building, from clay, paints, and Playmobile to Lincoln Logs, Pipe Works and Lego. They grew up with toys that would help them in their journey toward knowing how to imagine, design, and make things. Once they started school they also had their own tool belts with measuring tapes, screwdrivers and hammers. They helped Graeme with countless house remodeling projects. I encouraged them to use their imaginations and make up stories to play together.

This is not to say they were only creative and naturally nonviolent. The desire for power and control over others is a characteristic of our humanity. My 23-month-old once offered to help me with the newborn by "mammering" him. I waylaid the boy on his run to fix his crying brother with a wooden hammer. Another time, when my mom and dad were visiting our young family, they asked our boys where the wooden baseball bats that they had given them were. They answered with what sounded like, "A pie!" It wasn't until they took my parents into the kitchen that my folks realized the boys were actually saying, "Up high" to indicate the toys had been confiscated and put on top of the refrigerator out of reach. I didn't allow the boys to play baseball unsupervised until I was assured they understood that bats were to be used exclusively on baseballs and not brothers.

I began to recognize that my maternal influence for good might never make my little guys committed peacemakers. One day while I was standing at the sink as Andrew and Ryan were eating lunch, it became completely apparent that other influences might outweigh mine. I heard the sounds kids make with their mouths when imaginary bullets are flying, "Pew! Pew! Pew!" "Bang, bang, bang!" "Pow! Pow!" and turned around to discover that Andrew had chewed his sandwich into the shape of a revolver and Ryan had managed to bite off part of a pretzel to fashion a gun for himself. They had lost interest in eating and were shooting at each other.

Later that year, Graeme and I became unwitting accomplices in the boys' first toy guns acquisition when we told them they were free to spend the money they were earning doing extra chores on anything they wanted during our upcoming trip to Disneyland. It had never occurred to me that Disney was a toy arms dealer. Frontierland sold both rifles and six-shooters in holsters and New Orleans Square had an attractive supply of pirate's pistols. Not willing to go back on our word on something so long anticipated and earned, we came home from the happiest place on earth with a fully stocked arsenal.

Having failed to keep them unarmed, I wanted to give them a larger perspective than our popular culture offers by expanding the guys' understanding of things like weapons throughout history, the advantages of guns over trap hunting, the societal consequences of war, and learning about the lives of heroic people who had influenced the world for peace. Their Uncle Tom in Alaska told stories that included info about the best guns for protection from bears, and friends who were hunters gave them other perspectives on firearms.

When Braden was in his early teens, he took up the hobby of playing airsoft, a team sport using "toy" guns that shoot plastic pellets. I wasn't entirely caught off guard. I had noticed over the years that Braden had an obvious interest in military history and a mind that retained random details regarding vehicles, weaponry and other equipment used in war. He wasn't keen on any of the usual high school sports, but he liked being part of a team and had a heart for fairness and upholding the rights of the underdog. I could understand the sense of fun and adventure he and his buddies enjoyed on the airsoft fields because as a kid I had joined in the "citrus wars," where we neighborhood kids pelted each other with lemons, oranges and grapefruit from our trees while we shielded ourselves with the metal lids from the trash cans in the alley.

During college, Braden found a part-time sales job at a large retailer of airsoft guns and tactical apparel. Working with customers in the store gave him connections to other kids and adults in the world of airsoft. He learned about sales and marketing. He began playing more at local airsoft fields, where some of the games involved protecting unarmed civilians and rescuing hostages. He also met people in the military and law enforcement who practiced during training exercises with airsoft replicas of the firearms they used at work. He had discussions with experienced experts about active shooter scenarios and the relative merits and drawbacks of strategies like "Run, Hide, Fight" taught by different branches of the service and various law enforcement agencies.

While Braden has a degree in Television, Film and Media, he continues working in the airsoft business and has opened an airsoft field and retail store in Hawaii with his friends, Anthony, a Navy and Coast Guard commander and his wife, Teresa. Recently they had the fun of being part of production for *Jurassic World Exodus*, a popular fan film, securing locations, supplying extras, airsoft guns and other props. They're also working with the community, military, government agencies and law enforcement.

The interest and even passion some people have for guns and use of force as the best means for addressing human conflict is difficult for me to understand. I grew up hearing many of the adults in my life talk frankly about the irreparable harm and heartache caused by violence. It's easier for me to recognize the hope for humanity and nobility in the fight for nonviolence, forgiveness and self-sacrifice. I lived in the era of the peaceful protests of the Civil Rights Movement, Vietnam War and Woodstock. Having been on the receiving end of hostility during my high school years, perhaps I'm still sensitized to violence. I started my unplanned career in homeschooling in part because a second-grader brought a handgun to school.

At times, the world seems bent on violence and destruction. Like many of us, it grieves me to have to keep dialoguing about guns and the loss we suffer from school shootings, gang violence, terrorism, active shooters and war. These are heavy and complex subjects. It's stress-inducing and exhausting just thinking about how to ensure our peaceful self-government, increase national security, decide what is the necessary and appropriate use of force by police officers and what the role of our military abroad should be.

The internal conflict I experience regarding these kinds of issues frequently drives me to the edge of our continent to find the peace I feel near the ocean. I could happily spend the rest of my days hanging out with friends and family, watching the waves roll in, humming that potent and often maligned *Kumbaya* prayer together for the world. "Help, God. Come by here." We all need more of these times of refreshment and recalibration of heart in our places of natural beauty to move forward together in addressing and resolving these complex issues. Our world needs the benefit of our participation. Because of love, we must determine to keep our hearts engaged. I want a whole, kind and functional world to be a reality for future generations.

USO

Four Blackhawk helicopters waited on the tarmac, rotor blades rumbling as they churned up the warm air. Jill and Kate climbed off the plane. Jill was dismayed and Kate thrilled to find out their next gig was only a helicopter ride away.

These ladies are musicians who have had the opportunity to sing backup for top artists in arenas and stadiums and perform as a duo all over the world. They understand the joy and connection music creates for others. Music is both their profession and their contribution to making the world a better place.

In 2015, like many musicians and entertainers before them, they had the chance to perform for troops deployed in conflict zones with the United Service Organizations (USO). The experience was life-changing as they spent time hanging out with and encouraging Americans far from home. They said the simple exchanges they had with soldiers behind the scenes—next to hospital beds, in mess halls and moving around the different installations—seemed to them to be even more important and meaningful than their time on stage performing.

I often think we could really use USO-type shows of our own in the United States after disasters and other tragedies, for both the survivors and the army of people moving in to help. Almost always, our spirits need a boost to keep our efforts energized. Certain minstrels and comedians know how to find the right songs, sounds and stories to help us process our troubled emotions, make us laugh, and remind us of our shared humanity. There's a need to create the sense of hopeful possibility in the face of what appears impossible.

Treasure Hunt

Mom quietly shooed Dad, my 5-year-old sister Linda and me out of the little cabin in the Sierras so the baby could nap. Looking for something to do with us, Dad found an old bike in the shed and helped Linda get up and balance on the front handlebars. I climbed behind him on the back bumper and the three of us set off around Donner Lake to the shack of a country store to buy treats. It's funny what childhood memories linger like it was yesterday, while other details are lost and forgotten. This one I remember because it introduced treasure hunting as a family tradition.

After each of us picked out our own candy bar—quite a treat in the days when candy bars were shared and three pieces of penny candy was our normal weekly allowance— we headed back home along the rough dirt road. Laughing about balancing on the bike and trying to eat, Linda surprised us by starting to cry. Dad quickly stopped and I got off so we could find out what had gone wrong. Linda held up her white Big Hunk taffy bar and showed us a spot of bright red where she had been eating. Still crying, she opened her mouth to show us what was wrong. She had swallowed her first tooth. A tomboy, she wasn't hurt or grossed out. She was only crying because she was worried she'd miss getting the dime from the tooth fairy she'd seen me find under my pillow.

Dad reassured her things would work out. Linda wiped her tears and we climbed back on the bike. When we got back to the cabin, after Mom congratulated Linda, she helped her write a note to explain the Big Hunk incident to the tooth fairy. They went upstairs to our cots and put it under Linda's pillow before we got on with the rest of the day. Linda went to bed that night hoping the tooth fairy would understand.

The next morning, instead of the expected dime, Linda found a note with a penny taped to it. She handed it to me and I read, "Thank you for telling me about how you lost your tooth. Now <u>look</u> and see how cute you are without it! Signed, The Tooth Fairy."

We looked around the room and saw that the little, cracked mirror on the wall had a note taped to it with another penny, "How many steps does the attic ladder have?"

We climbed down, counting, and on the last one found another clue with a penny. We continued with one clue and penny leading to the next until Linda had ten cents, an amount that seemed like more money than the little dimes I had received. From that day on, we girls always left a note with the tooth under our pillows, asking for a treasure hunt.

Our ability to become resilient individually and together requires us to maintain a deliberate treasure-hunting mindset. In troubled times, it takes hopeful conviction to move in the direction of realizing practical solutions. We need to believe that fresh, positive outcomes can be found. Defensiveness and insistence on tradition can keep us from seeking new ways of thinking that lead from one discovery to the next.

The building blocks of most solutions rarely lie exclusively in one philosophical jurisdiction of power and control. We miss obvious treasure simply because it's "hidden" outside our customary way of thinking or our political group or religious faction. Wisdom often inhabits the space outside the certainty of what we think, in the mystery of what we don't know yet.

I've found that many people are unwilling to believe that there's anything of worth to be found in "a different camp." Not simply political, this conviction that the truth is "ours" and not "theirs" is found wherever there is an "us" and "them." For example, some scientists rationalize with precision why the realms of religion contain no essential, undiscovered elements, and some religious folks fastidiously abstain from studying the changes and transformation happening in the physical world around us.

Years ago, a group of friends was hanging out after dinner at our friend James' loft space in an old brewery, when he asked if we'd pray for him about the book he was writing, *God.com*. Standing around him, with the LA skyline in the background, we got quiet as different ones took a moment to pray encouragement, ask for wisdom on his behalf or suggest a thought that came to mind. Relaxed, I closed my eyes, and as I did something like a short film played out in my imagination. I saw a busy-body "church lady" dressed in old-fashioned finery, gray hair in a beehive updo, walk toward James. I watched as she handed him a beautiful velvet bag with a drawstring, like something a queen might have used in the Middle Ages for gold coins or treasure. I saw James take the bag, open it and almost immediately drop it in disgust. In my mind's eye,

I looked on the ground and saw the reason for his revulsion: spilling out of the bag was a pile of fresh manure. But I also saw what James couldn't, twinkling out from the dark mess, there were beautiful, brilliantly colored seeds that looked like gemstones.

I shared the daydream and this thought with James, "A lot of people never see the seeds that are hidden in fertilizer." That prompted James to tell a bit of his story. When he was a child, he had received a real mixed bag of lessons—religious and otherwise—from the people in his community. Many of us have. Most of life's wisdom presents itself in conditions that are less than pristine. Learning to see what's most important and holds the keys to future harvests requires a particular kind of fortitude. It's a mark of inner maturity to seek for the seeds of wisdom that are hidden in places that stink.

In 2014 our son Ryan wrote a music video treatment with a storyline about a treasure hunt that begins in a neighborhood in California and ends on a seaside bluff in Scotland. The songwriter Steven Curtis Chapman and his family were experiencing the severe pain and loss after the death of one of their children. The song, an inspirational anthem, *The Glorious Unfolding,* was written as encouragement to keep seeking when our hearts are breaking. In the video, a young woman is mourning her father's death and as she walks through his home, discovers he's left her clues to find a final message from him.

Steven used music to help process his grief and encourage his family. People who heard his song were encouraged in their own challenges and responded by sharing their stories of grief and renewed vision. The music video added another dimension, and as a result, even more people were heartened in their journeys.

In the face of heartache that comes from devastating tragedy and suffering, regaining a positive view of the future seldom just happens. It takes looking for the way that leads forward. It's rarely obvious or easy to see. To be willing to keep seeking fresh solutions requires reassurance that there's still good ahead, and, in the case of communities, it requires the ability to move past divisive thinking.

Music, film, story and other art forms bring unique inspiration to our search for treasure, especially in times when we are discouraged or disheartened. Perhaps the annual Grammy, Emmy, Tony and Academy Awards could consider presenting a Community Resilience Award for the efforts of writers, actors or other artists whose work has encouraged and inspired us in some way to be stronger and more resilient as individuals or as a nation. The creative arts have the rare ability to open our hearts and minds to possibilities and hint at a promising future hidden in the rubble of the present.

Day One

The screen in the dark theater exploded with noise and bright light, causing a shock to the senses and giving me a jolt of unexpected adrenaline. The images were blurred at first, deliberately creating a sense of confusion and disorientation. War veteran, screenwriter and director Henry Hughes was inviting us to experience a piece of his story, the daily traumas of war and the insights he gained through his background as a soldier in his Oscar-nominated movie, *Day One.*

One of the great beauties of books and the audio and visual arts is their amazing capacity to transport us from our daily lives to other geographies, cultures, times and even into the minds and hearts of other human beings. In Henry's story about a woman's first day working as a translator for a US Army unit in Afghanistan, we as an audience can actually undergo some of the emotions this woman and the other characters in the story are feeling if we allow our imaginations to engage us. We learn about others, not through some exacting academic or cognitive effort on our part but as visceral participants in human experience.

We're rarely able to be as dualistic in our thinking—I am right and you are wrong—when we've walked in the shoes of another, especially the shoes of one we have judged harshly from our own frame of reference. There is hidden potency in the frequently used tool of film, the Point of View shot, where the camera takes us into someone else's eyes and we're able to see the world as another views it.

In the first moments of his work, Henry offers the viewer the opportunity to become intimately acquainted with the translator's vulnerability and "otherness" from the male troops she will accompany. Henry said that as he was writing the script, he was thinking about the significance of the "female voice" in war. He related how the computer voice in a tank is female so that it stands out from the men's voices as they operate it. He recalled how a helicopter full of men suddenly grew quiet when a female pilot spoke over the radio. This contemplation of the female voice and his interactions with his own translator shaped his storytelling.

By the end of the movie, if we've imagined ourselves in the position of the various characters as they have faced unexpected and harsh circumstances, we've felt the emotions and challenges that the civilians and soldiers have experienced. We may have even viscerally understood the profound contrasts between the male and female perspectives on war.

A movie just might be a vehicle for giving and receiving the gift of empathy.

Free Americans

"Hey, Mom and Dad, where are you guys? I just got back to the house and we've had a break in."

Andrew's call reached Graeme and me as we were going into our first meeting at a small business event at the Pasadena Convention Center one morning. We had driven out of our driveway only 45 minutes earlier, so the thieves must have been in and out quickly.

When we got there we walked through the house feeling dismayed by the evidence of the burglars. Every room in the house had drawers opened with many of them turned upside down and the contents spread on the floor. What gold jewelry we had was gone. We moved through rooms, trying to assess all the technology that had been taken. In the chaos, it was hard to remember where things were kept and what was missing as the police asked for an inventory and description of stolen items. It was hard to know what to do next once the police left. This wasn't the way we had planned to spend the day.

Over the next week as we fixed the broken window and tried to restore order to the house, we discovered more items that had been stolen. The sense of violation of our personal life grew as some of our things were found in another part of town, discarded in an alley. Items that had been meaningful and valuable to us, ruined because people who had no right had taken what was ours. It took weeks for things to get back to normal. Even with insurance, there was no way to fully restore everything we had lost to thieves.

My parents remember the sense of horror and fear that permeated California after the 1941 attack on Pearl Harbor. My mom, who was 7 years old, recalls her mother crying as they heard on the radio that Hawaii had been bombed. The rest of December, usually happy as Christmas approached, was filled instead with dread and uncertainty.

By February, a new normal had become routine. My mom's dad would leave the house at dusk and go from house to house as the block warden, making sure that everyone on the street had pulled their window shades down and no lights could be seen from the air. But, on February 19, 1942, President Roosevelt issued an executive order that all people of Japanese ancestry in the United States were to be placed in concentration camps. Mom says she remembers her mother crying and being distraught when she discovered their friends, Iti and Tru, and their three children had been given 24 hours to pack suitcases with everything they would "need" for an indeterminate length of time.

These family friends were sent to the Santa Anita Racetrack Assembly Center, forced to live in reeking, recently vacated horse stalls before eventually being relocated to an internment camp in the desert. Like people fleeing a disaster with little notice, Japanese Americans had to leave their comfortable homes, all their furniture, household items, family mementoes and friends, not knowing if or when they would be allowed to come back. Fear and prejudice created a disaster for about 70,000 Americans and another 50,000 legal immigrants.

Mom doesn't remember the ways her parents might have helped their friends during the war, but she knows my grandfather made sure Iti was treated kindly when their family was finally allowed to move home from the camp and were trying to get back on their feet. Granddad Brockman helped him get his job back at the dairy where they had worked together before the war. This family's story was excruciatingly painful and full of immeasurable losses. Other families suffered as much and worse. Many lost loved ones, had their property stolen, and were unable to return to past jobs. Most had to build entirely new lives after the war.

My dad's recollections of life during WWII are different from my mom's. As a 10-year-old, he remembers wondering if it was only a matter of time before the Japanese would attack California. But, Dad says he was completely unaware of the imprisonment of Americans of Japanese descent. He knows now that his parents must have known, but he doesn't recall them talking about it or trying to help. It wasn't until after the war when Dad became friends at school with kids who had come back from the various concentration camps that he learned about the injustice of what they had been through.

I have many Japanese American friends whose families were imprisoned during World War II. Those families were irrevocably changed. They lost every remnant of the lives they had believed in and known as free Americans. They were the victims of crimes against them that lasted for years, continued after they were released and of a nature far more devastating than any simple burglary. Yet, often these disgraceful events are barely a footnote in many people's understanding of America, an unfocused and far-distant past for those whose families did not endure the indignity and hardships of internment. Some white Americans still believe their fellow Americans who were imprisoned deserved what they got. Yet, the loss of possessions, property, livelihoods and basic human rights are the childhood memories of many of my friends' parents. These American concentration camps still represent legacies of family heartache.

Our friend Jon grew up knowing that his grandparents had suffered the loss of their successful businesses when they were interned with their children. His grandfather was imprisoned and treated as a war criminal simply for being a store owner who mostly served the Japanese-American community. He was imprisoned separately from his family and contracted Valley Fever. He was given inadequate care and eventually sent to a hospital in a freight car on a train, forced to stand for the journey. Jon only heard this story when his own father was in the hospital and his dad's older sister related how they had been allowed out of the camp for a visit to see their father before he died. The betrayal they experienced by their government cannot be underestimated. These families were deeply traumatized as a result of what they lost because our government treated her citizens in defiance of their rights and our constitution.

As a child, I heard many stories like these from family friends in our neighborhood, an older couple, Herbert and Madeline Nicholson. Having lived and worked in Japan as missionaries for decades before the war, they felt a deep connection to those who abruptly and unjustly lost everything in the name of national security. They helped convert a church building into a makeshift storage unit so Japanese families had somewhere to store their household possessions that friends like my grandfather were able to save for them. Uncle Herbie, as many called him, actively sought to mediate the injustice of forced internment by going to Washington to lobby for the civil rights of the Japanese American community. Failing to bring an end to the imprisonment, he and Madeline represented as best they could the remaining assets and interests of Japanese businesspeople and families in Los Angeles. They traveled back and forth to Manzanar and other internment camps logging thousands of miles during the years of the war.

By being able to hear Uncle Herbie's stories about those years, we came to realize how extensive were the unseen losses America suffered as well with the internment of these citizens. As a nation we suffered the loss of their skills, involvement in the economy and, most importantly, their compassionate contributions to our communities. These Americans returned, changed by the exclusion, theft and hatred they had experienced at the hands of their countrymen.

We hurt everyone when we choose to fearfully and blindly accept decisions by those in authority who judge, without representation and due process, the people in our world. We are a country that, whether intentionally or not, declared at our inception that we believed all people are created equal. We pledge allegiance to a flag that we say represents justice for all. We must adhere to these higher standards if we are to endure and thrive. We must continue with intention and learn from the error of our ways.

Sadly, the term "Ugly American" is often apparent not simply in the behavior of some of us abroad, but in the way we treat each other here at home. A groundswell of people caring and speaking up for the rights of all Americans will contribute to our strength as a society and our resilience as a nation. There is a powerful and intrinsic possibility in the ideals expressed in our founding documents and aspects of our history that we have never fully committed to with heart and action. We need to move forward with a love that's willing to take action with and for our neighbors.

Empowered
Female Silhouette

"Okay! I'll get to the gym while you guys go for a run. Meet me back here in a couple hours and we can all go to lunch."

Our three sons were in New York, visiting from Los Angeles and Nashville, and the four of us had spent most of the morning having breakfast and catching up while Graeme was at the Joint Field Office (JFO) in Queens. I jumped up out of the chair where I had been sitting, failing to notice until the moment I landed that my left leg had fallen asleep. My full weight came to rest for an excruciating few seconds on the outside of my ankle. Searing pain and the swelling red, black and blue coloring told me I had done real damage.

Not a great injury story for people who asked in the following couple of months, "So, how did you break your ankle?"

"I got out of my chair wrong."

"Really. Wow. Really? Just stood up?"

"Yep. Just stood up."

"Were you wearing heels?"

"Nope. No. Tennis shoes. Leg was asleep."

"Really? Well. Hmm. So sorry."

I have friends who delight in wearing high heels, but heels have rarely been my shoe of choice. After recovering from my injury, I was even more determined to keep my feet firmly planted on the ground, especially tackling the streets and subways of New York. The shock of having my leg twist under me made a permanent impression like the classical conditioning experiment where Pavlov's dogs salivated just at the sound of their dinner bell. Simply the sight of other women walking in heels recalled the pain in my ankle.

A few years back, I took three friends from the Netherlands to a Hollywood studio so they could see a live recording of a television show. It happened to be a talk show with a cast of doctors offering advice based on their knowledge of medicine. I recall it was the unanimous opinion of the doctors that high heels had health benefits for women, citing muscular development, the tilt of the pelvis and "the empowered female silhouette." I remember all of us laughing as we drove back home, deciding we should each skip buying gym memberships and just invest in a nice pair of stilettos and walk laps around our neighborhoods. We joked about Hollywood's depictions of female spies, detectives and superheroes running after bad guys in heels, scaring villains with their powerful silhouettes. We concluded that there was something more afoot than the doctors' concern for women's health.

From my perspective, there's an inordinate amount of attention in American culture given to what women choose to wear, as if clothing or a woman's appearance can determine if she's intelligent, qualified, or capable. Assessing someone's IQ or insight based on what they look like or happen to be wearing is rather like judging whether or not I'm a good writer based on my dancing skills. I'm disinclined to believe that the statistical probability of a woman's value to our community is reflected in her style of dress or the height of her shoes.

I remember my dad coming home from Jet Propulsion Laboratory after a promotion that involved moving to the executive floor near the lab director's office. Dad always wore a coat and tie to work, but said he thought he might need to step things up given his new position. With his usual dry wit, he told us he'd go shopping over the weekend for Bermuda shorts and the kind of sandals that looked good with socks. Turns out the director was a nerdy scientist with a disregard for the adage that clothes make the man. They don't make the woman either.

After Katrina, when we attended the Natural Hazards Workshop, we heard for the first time about the huge implications of the way our culture continues to arbitrarily assess a woman's value, credibility and responsibilities. The issues of equality that exist between men and women are glaringly apparent in disaster. Since the needs of women during response and recovery are categorically different from men's and frequently overlooked or disregarded, there are far-reaching consequences to the community at large.

There is a preponderance of research indicating that while women work hard at communicating accurately their assessments of their own needs and the needs of their family and community after disasters, their voices are often drowned out within the response and recovery chaos. As a result, the specific aid required for the female half of the population to bounce back and get on their feet is severely lacking.

At the workshop, we got the opportunity to get to know many different researchers doing work in the field of disaster and its intersection with gender, and the interesting differences in the ways women and men experience crisis. Over the years, we've stayed in touch with two of the researchers whose work made a lasting impression on us, Roxane Richter, Ph.D. and Elaine Enarson, Ph.D.

Roxane, a social scientist, international aid worker, author, healthcare communications specialist and emergency medical technician reported to the Houston convention center in September 2005 to offer help as an American Red Cross Disaster Health Services volunteer. She described the confusion and "congealing mayhem" as local Houston first responders were quickly overwhelmed with the needs of survivors when over 200,000 evacuees from Katrina began to arrive.

We were surprised to learn from Roxane and others working in the trenches of response that crucial medical supplies for women are seldom made a priority. For example, Roxane described how she tried to administer appropriate care to women in health crises without the necessary OB/GYN equipment, supplies or the basic medicines women require. They simply weren't a part of standard operating procedure.

In a disaster like Katrina, the exclusion of women's input and decision making power is especially obvious and irrational. Female anatomy, more open to infections, suffers disproportionately when wading waist deep in toxic flood waters full of sewage, oil and corpses. It makes no sense that half of the population is treated as though these specific considerations are surprising. Pregnant women and nursing mothers, who make it safely away from the natural hazard, experience a personal and inexcusable collateral disaster when they do not receive the immediate care they need, having their health or the health of their child severely compromised.

We heard from many that while there was ample soap, toothbrushes, toothpaste, deodorant, razors, diapers and formula after Katrina, supply shipments didn't contain feminine napkins or tampons. Every woman I know considers sanitary supplies more crucial than toothpaste when she's on her period. Yet the powers that be failed to include them. Many volunteers working at various shelters related accounts of long drives made in search of necessary feminine supplies. When they could be found, they would buy as much as possible, load them in cars and vans, and return to the disaster area. This is a huge amount of extra effort at the expense of all those giving or receiving crucial aid, yet the need is entirely predictable.

We heard stories of women traumatized by having to choose between their own emergency care and their children's or elderly parents' wellbeing. It was a no-win situation. Women, who statistically most often fill the vital role of family caregiver, were not viewed as having actual jobs that were important to the essential needs of the community. Sociological research has shown "women's work" is both intrinsic to the strength of any culture's fabric—and completely undervalued. Families and communities suffer when we practice disaster response and recovery without an intelligent and informed understanding of all our needs. We require official strategies to powerfully support women and their huge contribution to society.

Roxane related how after her work during the Katrina response she informed a FEMA executive about the discrepancies and how other nations deliberately include women, their voluntary work and their gender-specific needs in official disaster planning. He replied that we do, too, and that if Roxane was interested in learning more about how women were included she should contact FEMA's Disability Office. As it turned out, women—half of our country's population and workforce—were relegated to a demographic subset on our government's emergency management organizational chart. Roxane was incredulous and responded, "We're not disabled. We are women."

Academics and practitioners continue to wonder what it will require for the simple and practical applications from disaster research and experience to finally be given the priority they deserve and integrated into the way we "do disasters."

Our colleague Elaine has extensive experience as a disaster expert, professor, author, editor and activist. She was initiated into the world of disaster as a young mother shortly after their family's move to Florida while her husband was in Australia on business. She was shocked by the disruption Hurricane Andrew caused in her life and became interested in researching the unique ways men and women suffer and survive disaster.

Elaine's research affirms that men and women perceive risk differently, prioritize differently, respond differently to threats to their family's safety and have different strengths and weaknesses when it comes to our contributions to community recovery. Elaine and others have worked to interest disaster response agencies and organizations in using the research available about the differences between women's and men's experiences, but this overarching issue remains largely unaddressed.

It's important that we as a nation change the focus of our attention from the "female silhouette" to the actual presence of women on every board, executive team and decision-making body. We need a proportionate representation of women, and when we don't have it, we need to recognize there are many profound and negative implications for all of us. It's time as a nation to see that we require the presence of both female and male influence and authority for all of us to thrive in day-to-day life as well as recover from crises. The essential contributions of women are important and we need to ensure we can all hear female voices in every arena of society.

Feasts and Floods

When Graeme and I live in different places around the country, we like to visit different houses of worship to have a better understanding of the community's life and make friends where we can. On this visit, the rector's voice echoed in the old church building as he spoke of different losses sustained by the people of his community during the historic floods of 2016 in the Baton Rouge region of Louisiana. The beauty of sunlight shining through the old stained glass contrasted with the mental images he created as he described floodwaters invading homes, water lapping against cabinetry and furniture, and the loss of photos and other precious family heirlooms as piles of debris grew along streets.

As the rector began to share about the ways people in the parish had given their time to help others, he mentioned an image he said was especially indicative of Louisianans—two men, smiles on their faces, standing in water up to their knees, working an oversized grill, loaded with meat as they cooked for their community. He laughed as he said, "Our community knows what's important when all is said and done. It's the people… and it's the food!" His comment brought a ripple of laughing agreement and head nodding.

In the days following, as the waters receded, the first stages of recovery continued with people gutting their homes in hopes of keeping mold from growing. The on-going theme of barbecues, grills and smokers played a central role in keeping the community going.

Eating is obviously essential to sustaining life, but eating good food together during difficult times creates an atmosphere of communion that builds a sense of communal resilience. More than just people's physical bodies are sustained by a meal. I learned this as a child.

Though we ate well as a family and had lots of fun with a variety of people around our family table, we needed to learn about feasting from others. In the words of the Greek papa in *My Big Fat Greek Wedding*, "These people are toast with no jam." Our family's basic food culture was similar. The amount of food prepared was adequate but not necessarily bountiful or lavish. It was because of friends, teaching us by example over the years, that we learned the power and importance of heaping the figurative jam on toast, piling quantities of the good stuff high on our communal tables.

We learned the importance of celebrating with bounty from our family's many Armenian friends. Accustomed to marking every significant life event with their extended family and friends gathered around food, they set the bar for how we all came together.

As a child, I remember the mouthwatering smell of barbecuing shish-kebab floating down past river-rock walls in Farnsworth Park where we kids were playing softball, making it hard to concentrate on the game. We played with one eye on the ball and the other eye up the hill, trying to gauge how much longer we had to wait for lunch, watching our mothers load potluck side dishes on the checkered tablecloths as our dads finished grilling platters of barbecued meat and vegetables. We kids would wrap up our game, run up the hill and enjoy the sense of fun that happens with great food around a family table.

These kinds of celebrations created a sense of multi-generational community even though we weren't next-door neighbors. I got to know not just my peers but their parents as well, as they helped serve up food, talked around the tables and encouraged us to eat heartily.

Years later when Graeme and I moved back to Pasadena with our boys to work on the Northridge earthquake recovery, I renewed a friendship with Sheri, a childhood friend from those days of picnicking. My parents were friends with Sheri's parents, who were first-generation Americans. Their parents, Sheri's grandparents, emigrated from Armenia, bringing the warm hospitality of their culture with them. My family benefitted.

As our boys grew up, we became reacquainted with this magical power of food to build community. Sheri, Matt, and their six kids lived within walking distance in our neighborhood and we frequently shared impromptu dinners around their big dining room table. During those years, many of us began offering that same easy hospitality ourselves, with everyone pitching in to make meals together happen often. The menus were rarely restaurant or cookbook worthy, although sometimes we'd be surprised by the coordinated bounty we'd pull from our various refrigerators and cupboards, combining them on someone's kitchen table, a potluck in the true sense of the word. We learned through experience that frequently sharing meals together builds community and is its own form of emergency preparedness.

When it rains in Southern California it can quickly become a disaster, with soil, packed and dry from months of no rain, unable to absorb, water sheets off and can flood roads, cause landslides especially where wildfires have burned through and in general overflow drainage capacities in our cities. One year when the rains came fast and furious, we got a call for help late one night from our friends, the Halberts, who lived in the foothills of Burbank. Their pool was overflowing, threatening to pour into their family room, kitchen and living room, at the same time rain was coming through windows in their second-story remodel. Their house was in danger of being permanently damaged if they didn't get help. Not long after Graeme and Braden showed up to siphon the pool and cover the windows and other friends came to help mop up the house, Sheri arrived with hot soup. What began as a disaster became a memory of happy camaraderie because we had already built community.

Pull Up a Chair

In the early mornings while living in Baton Rouge, I would walk around City Park, the golf course and the lakes. I generally said a good morning to the people I passed, and on occasion exchanged a few words about the day, the weather or their golf game. Living in a variety of places around the country, far from family and friends, I've learned to enjoy a bit of conversation wherever it's offered.

I was walking slowly around the lake early one hot August morning not long after we arrived, trying to adjust to the unfamiliar humidity when a woman I said good morning to responded with, "It's so hot!"

"It sure is compared to home! Will I get used to this?"

"No! It's too hot to get used to. Where are you from?"

By this time, we were each walking backward, having passed each other as we continued in opposite directions.

My answer of, "California!" caused enough connection for her to turn around and join me. As it turned out, she and her husband had recently bought a second home near Santa Barbara not far from ours in California. In our first walk together I found out her name was Juan Li Vignes, she was originally from China, had married her husband 12 years before and their home on University Lake had been used for scenes in the *Pitch Perfect* films.

In the simple way that friendships form, we found we had more in common as she asked me about living in California and told me about her life in Baton Rouge. We became walking buddies, adjusting our routes to meet up and enjoy each other's company.

After some weeks, Juan Li asked if I could join her and a friend for lunch to celebrate Mooncake Day, a Chinese autumn tradition of getting together with family and friends to celebrate and share a meal. When I arrived at the restaurant I had the pleasant surprise of sharing lunch with five additional women and one of their grandsons.

The women mostly spoke Cantonese with each other that day, catching one another up on friends and family and making sure I always had food on my plate and was enjoying the different flavors. Food makes a way for human connections to happen. I've found over the years that I don't have to understand what everyone is saying to feel included in the circle. To simply have a seat at a table where friends are laughing and talking and enjoying good food is a privilege. Unexpectedly, one of Juan Li's friends, Cathy, took the bill and insisted on paying for all of us. I have a strong sense of gratitude to this circle of women who, having made Louisiana their home, chose to make me feel welcomed in a state far from my home. A willingness to include strangers at our tables, in our celebrations and in meals out with friends is a simple way to build connections within our communities and the resilience that comes with them.

My friend Renee Guilbault oversaw Food and Beverage for an international bakery and restaurant brand that originated in Belgium. Besides the traditional, rustic breads and other menu items, Renee's friend Alain Coumont the brand's founder, made certain that a central feature of his business franchise was the communal table like the one he put in his first bakery shop in Brussels. A large, communal table in a restaurant can become a place of connection for both neighbors and strangers. It's possible for businesses to help us create these opportunities for connection.

When Graeme and I were living in New York City after Hurricane Sandy it was difficult to meet people and make friends. One rainy day I was on a lunch break in the cafeteria downstairs, which had an interesting variety of different food stations. I had assembled my lunch from the salad bar and found a seat at a long table that faced out the front windows. A young woman came and sat next to me in the packed restaurant with a steaming bowl of noodles, broth, chicken and vegetables. The smell was enticing and her enjoyment of her meal was obvious. I struck up a conversation with her about what station her noodles were from and what ingredients she liked best.

It wasn't long before I had discovered Michelle worked at New York City's tourist bureau, was first-generation Chinese American, and would be graduating from college soon. We enjoyed each other's company enough that day to meet several more times at the cafeteria to share lunch and anecdotes from our lives. Over time, I heard a bit about her family's remodel project and we discussed the merits of different flooring. She heard about our adjustment to living in New York City and offered advice about commuting around town. We talked about careers and the opportunities she was interested in and the things I had learned over my lifetime. Michelle, more than any of the tourist attractions she told me about, became one of the highlights of my time spent in New York.

After Hurricane Harvey, I would take my computer some days and work at a coffee shop in Houston. One of the features that I appreciated, besides the delicious coffee, was that the owner, Ozguzhan, created a space that felt welcoming. In addition to cafe tables, there was a conversation circle of sofa and chairs and a communal table made by simply pushing two tables together that seats eight. Add to that, Ozzie was friendly and outgoing and helped the neighborhood feel at home in his shop, sharing stories about life in Turkey and his travels in the navy.

Ultimately, it's the intentions of our hearts and the small actions of friendly connection we share that will shape our overall strength as a nation. The good that comes of simply hanging out in our public spaces with others who are different from us contributes powerfully to our overall resilience.

Acting Like Neighbors

We had been living in Louisiana for over a month, working on the March floods, when we went to Oregon for a family wedding. Unexpectedly during that time, Baton Rouge experienced swift, devastating and historic flooding from a storm that didn't look like trouble to the meteorologists until it failed to move through. The rain clouds lingered over the region and dumped an unprecedented amount of water. In hours, old rainfall records were shattered and neighborhoods that had never flooded required emergency boat evacuations.

If it weren't for fellow citizens stepping up to help, it's likely many more than 13 would have drowned trying to escape their homes. These citizen volunteers with boats dubbed themselves the Cajun Navy. People all over the region were rescued by surprisingly efficient ragtag teams of neighbors coordinated by phone, social media and word of mouth. Even folks from Mississippi showed up in force with their boats to help their neighbors in Louisiana get to dry land.

We returned to a city gasping from the loss of lives and the shock of having their familiar landscape, houses, cars, schools, businesses and sense of place unexpectedly disappear under water. The hotel where we were staying became a temporary refuge for the displaced, including some hotel employees and their families who had lost homes in the flood. The parking lot filled with cars full of what little could be salvaged, and the three washing machines for guests in the building were occupied around the clock, cleaning clothes that had been pulled sodden and polluted from dressers and closets awash in floodwater.

In the mornings as we left for work and in the evenings as we returned, we interacted with people in the halls, breakfast room, lobby and parking lot. We heard stories of their losses and the work they were doing to recover from devastation and bring their lives back to a semblance of normal. We found an organization, Together Baton Rouge, which was raising money to hire and train local workers in demolition and construction skills, hoping for some good to come from employing people who needed the work to begin the huge recovery ahead.

The attitude of most of the people we met in Baton Rouge who suffered loss from the flood was doggedly optimistic. They were determined to get back on their feet and be grateful for what they had in the process. As we worked and moved around the city, we found churches providing food banks and coordinating construction teams, people volunteering to house relatives, pull out drywall, prepare meals, foster pets, run errands, help with childcare, lend an ear and offer encouragement. We were often thanked and uplifted by those who had every reason to be preoccupied with their own troubles. We saw firsthand how many ways there are within a caring community to be neighborly and contribute to disaster recovery.

The plane was only partially full when the doors closed, ready for takeoff. I was headed back to Baton Rouge after a trip home, happy there would be an open seat between the next passenger and me. I turned to her, thinking to briefly celebrate the extra space we had and the two of us didn't stop talking for the entire trip from Los Angeles to Louisiana. In just the first few minutes I found out that we had quite a few differences of opinion. I also found out that my seatmate Dianne was not afraid of controversy and was ready to discuss those differences with good-natured vigor. She set out immediately to wrangle me to her way of seeing things with a litany of facts. We had fun as the hours flew by.

As we talked, I found out Dianne was deeply invested in trying to inspire positive change in the people of Louisiana. Although she's a busy healthcare business owner, she's passionate about giving back to the community by putting on a cable talk show, *Dianne Andrews in Black and White*. She brings her unique energy and perspective to interviewing an interesting variety of guests, wanting to help her neighbors in Louisiana understand current issues and relevant history. Her interviews about the crimes committed by the Ku Klux Klan during the 1960s are especially intriguing. But it's Dianne's heart to facilitate understanding, build connections and try to heal old wounds I especially appreciate. She's a character, and we enjoyed our shared meals and conversations over the months that Graeme and I were working in Baton Rouge.

There are as many ways as there are people to be a good neighbor. Everyone doesn't need to be or do the same things to contribute to their community's resilience. If we follow our interests and passions and are willing to use our natural abilities and the variety of skills we've acquired for the good of our neighbors, we'll discover new ways to be stronger together.

Angola Prison

A small group of us from the Baton Rouge "Popcorn and Peace" class we'd been attending for several weeks drove through the gates into Angola Prison. Charlie deGravelles, who wears many hats, among them author, high school teacher, Episcopal deacon, gifted musician, and activist had been leading a series of evening classes for the community on topics like poverty, foster care, racial discrimination, corporate tax exemptions, crime reduction and the prison system. He wanted to create an environment for community learning and make space for discussion on sensitive topics that divided people in Baton Rouge and Louisiana. Charlie extended an invitation to anyone who was interested to spend a day at Angola.

Charlie had been volunteering for years, investing time and friendship in the lives of imprisoned men there. It was his hope that we would gain a greater understanding of the prison system and the changes that are needed by touring the facility and listening to some of the men share their stories. We walked through another series of gates and into one of several camps within the 18,000 acres of ranch and farmland to a chapel and the adjacent infirmary where a hospice program is located for men who are ill and living out their last days in prison.

We sat together in the pews to listen and learn a bit from different inmates about their daily routines and, in general, to gain a better understanding from their perspectives. Kerry Myers, the editor of *The Angolite*, an award-winning prison news magazine staffed by inmates, related some of his experiences and the wide-ranging stories he and others have covered. He told us his researched opinions about the clemency and commutation process that's in need of reform nationwide, explaining racial inequities and the ways that business and profit-making influence decisions.

We also heard from the men who worked in the hospice program. Beautiful quilts hung on the walls and an inmate explained their importance, showing us a quilt he was currently working on that would be used to cover a casket in the horse-drawn hearse used for prison funerals. Others told stories about what it was like to nurse and care for the dying and the deeply challenging aspects of that work. One man shared about his initial abhorrence of the intimate task of cleaning another man's body and related the gradual way his heart was tenderized as he served as caregiver to a fellow inmate who was suffering. He said that the process of learning to alleviate another's pain and discomfort had done more good in him than he had thought possible. Those who wear the t-shirts that identify hospice volunteers are respected within the prison population as being men who are growing in compassion for others as they work to address their own issues, regrets and pain.

After we spent time with the hospice patients, Charlie paused with our group in the dental clinic. He had recently written a book, *Billy Cannon: A Long, Long Run* about Angola's staff dentist, who had done time in the Federal Correctional Institute, Texarkana for counterfeiting $50 million and had been a former All-American football running back. As the others talked together with Charlie and Billy about the book, the staff nurse introduced me to Albert, the president of the inmate hospice program, and I had the opportunity to learn more from him.

I asked Albert what stirred his initial interest in hospice and what his thoughts were as he cared for the dying. He answered by telling me his story. I don't remember all of it accurately enough to write it here, but what I do recall is his sense of regret for the choices he made as a younger man. He described a childhood that left him susceptible to manipulation. He became calloused and unfeeling and said it took years before he came to realize that killing someone doesn't just destroy one life but many.

Albert's experiences had taught him the hard way that every life is valuable. There are circles of lives around each of us, and harming one life harms all the people who care about that person. He also recognized that he had inadvertently harmed all those who cared about him as well. As we talked he mentioned other aspects of life in Angola that have been impacted by his personal growth—his ability to earn money for his family working in the shop on his own time, the communication he has with his children, and a few of the meaningful relationships he has with other inmates and staff. He said working in hospice gives him something he needs.

Although being in Angola was a hard experience, I was unexpectedly encouraged by the human compassion I witnessed. I left with a sense of everyone's humanity and the importance of every individual, even those who are locked away. I left being able to see how there are circles of lives around all of us, including the incarcerated. Caring for them and finding ways to help them grow influences all of those connected to them, both in prison and in the larger community.

A Christian, a Jew and a Muslim Walk into a Library...

A small group of black and white adults slowly drifted into the community room in the public library one hot night in late spring 2017. Reverend Robin McCullough-Bade, the director of Baton Rouge's Interfaith Federation, welcomed each of us and encouraged us to make a name tag and help ourselves to iced tea and snacks. We found places around the tables she had pushed together to make one large circle and waited to see what was next. When Graeme and I are living in different parts of the country for months at a time working on disaster recovery, we search for ways to connect with locals, make friends and gain a deeper understanding of the communities we're seeking to serve. In Louisiana, where historic plantations with their constant reminders of the abuses of slavery are major tourist attractions, we wanted to learn what we could about how racial history might still be affecting people's thinking.

Graeme and I had originally connected with Robin at the Popcorn and Peace events in discussions about community healing and reconciliation. When we found out she was developing a small group curriculum for the Evangelical Lutheran Church in America (ELCA) on racial reconciliation we were interested. The project had come after a series of listening events the Interfaith Federation had encouraged in libraries around the city. Caring volunteers would simply be available at the "listening post" to listen to anything members of the community wanted to process or talk about following the Alton Sterling shooting and the floods.

As a result of the positive feedback from those events, she had decided to give the racial reconciliation curriculum a test run before she sent it on to ELCA, and had posted open invitations to the public at a couple of library locations so she could get input. Robin had written from her own perspective and wanted to hear other people's thoughts. She gave those of us who came to the different meetings opportunities to share our stories about how interracial relationships had shaped our lives or were currently impacting our experiences in Baton Rouge.

I also took an extension course through Louisiana State University that Robin taught on understanding the Abrahamic origins of Judaism, Islam and Christianity, another chance to gain a broader understanding of the people of Baton Rouge. We read passages from Jewish scriptures, the Quran and the New Testament.

We attended afternoon prayers at a mosque and went to a service at a local synagogue and had the opportunity to ask questions of leaders and members about their faith practices. Since most of us had been raised in the Christian faith, the experiences were enlightening and gave us the chance to interact with people from traditions that differed from ours.

Over the year we lived in Louisiana we saw a variety of ways people were deliberately growing peaceful and caring relationships across places where divisions exist. One of the events that the Interfaith Federation has hosted since 1990 is the "Sounds of CommUNITY Concert." In Louisiana, as is true in many communities in the United States, churches are mostly segregated by race in their attendance. For the concert in Baton Rouge, churches paired up to perform with a different denomination and, in many cases, with a church of a different racial composition.

There was humor and some tension evident behind the scenes at the 27th annual concert because the groups hadn't had much time to practice and were having to improvise together. But the point of the event wasn't lost as songs like "Let There Be Peace on Earth" and John Newton's "Amazing Grace" were performed.

Music events that deliberately seek to bridge diversity, mix things up and get people together, both to perform and be entertained, are valuable for our communities. Several years ago, Graeme and I went to a great concert with both Earth Wind and Fire and Chicago in downtown Los Angeles when they were on tour together. Because one band was black and the other mostly white, the crowd was happily diverse. It was a fun night and it felt wonderful to be sharing the space and the joy of music together. The same thing happens at many sporting events.

It's not those things that make us unique and distinguish us from each other that divide us. It's the negative attitudes we develop and defend about our diversity that create and reinforce our disconnections. We can learn a better way. Creating positive opportunities to draw people together will help us undo those prejudices. We can grow to actually enjoy each other by deliberately participating in experiences that are interesting or entertaining with people who are different from us.

Synagogue Tour

I was walking on Lexington near our apartment in New York City one day during the Hurricane Sandy recovery in 2013 when I noticed a plaque on a beautiful old building offering free tours of the sanctuary. The next Wednesday, I climbed several steps from the street, pushed open the heavy door and stepped into the cool and quiet foyer just in time to join the group of about twelve standing in a circle around a smartly dressed woman in her eighties. Bernice introduced herself, welcomed us and began to tell us about the history of the architecturally significant Central Synagogue.

As we moved through the different rooms, Bernice drew our attention to aspects of the building, how various features like the impressive pipe organ contributed to the worship services held there and pointed out the artistry of the tile work, stained glass and furniture design. The tour included the social hall in the basement and we heard a few anecdotes about the variety of events she had enjoyed there over the years.

By giving us a tour of the building where she worshipped, Bernice was inviting us to understand some of the things about her faith that were special to her. I left feeling my own appreciation for her synagogue because I had spent time enjoying its historical beauty. I felt a sense of connection with the people who worshipped there through Bernice's stories as she explained her own connections to her community and this place.

Later that day, I happened to glance up as I was picking out apples at a nearby grocery store and saw Bernice walking by in the produce section. I reintroduced myself and told her how much I had enjoyed her tour. We stood talking a bit about the things newly acquainted neighbors do in any small town, and we parted with each other's email addresses.

Over the next months, Bernice offered us tickets to an event she couldn't attend, and I dropped off some flowers. We met for lunch to get better acquainted and I called to ask her about local restaurants. Graeme and I got to enjoy our Valentine's dinner at one of her favorite spots in the neighborhood. Meeting Bernice helped Manhattan seem more like our home during the months we lived there.

Bernice and I are from different generations, different parts of the country, different faiths, and have differences of opinion. But because our paths crossed briefly at her place of worship, we found simple things we held in common—our grocery store, motherhood, foods we enjoy, flowers, music and museums.

Not all congregations meet in beautiful old buildings worthy of touring, but there are many different attributes of faith communities that could be shared. Some offer tutoring for neighborhood students, others teach English and life skills to new immigrants and some put on concerts open to the public. One of the easiest ways relationships are formed is through learning and growing together.

Perhaps it's possible for more of us to share the histories and traditions of our celebrations without an agenda to convert or recruit but with a simple desire to create understanding. Being willing as a faith community to show some form of hospitality to people in your neighborhood or accepting an invitation to enjoy a holiday celebration different from your own traditions are ways to build positive connections that bridge our differences.

Kindred Spirits

The sun was setting and the mountains above Pasadena were turning shades of rose and purple as John Muir High School's class of 1976 gathered on the large patio to celebrate 40 years. Doing what old friends do, we ate, drank, and reminisced. As the night progressed, we danced to songs from back in the day. Graeme had just moved to Louisiana to work on the 2016 flood recovery, so I went with Debbie and Claudia, high school buddies, feeling as though we had stepped back in time, immersed in childhood friendships. Partway through the night, our awesome drum corps showed up and the historic rhythms, pounding into the night, brought a flood of memories: days on the quad, pep assemblies in the auditorium, and football games played around Los Angeles and in the Rose Bowl where Muir faces rival Pasadena High every year in the November Turkey Tussle.

The first day I was bused across town against my will for my sophomore year in 1973, I felt a bit edgy and resistant about having to attend Muir. Fortunately for me, students on campus seemed generally more accepting than they had at Pasadena High and I felt unexpectedly comfortable the first few days. That sense of ease was complimented by the additional reassurance I was surprised to feel because I was walking the same halls my mother and aunts had as high school students. This new geography was a part of my family history.

But all that sense of safety drained away on my first Friday morning on campus. It just so happened that instead of riding the bus, Dad was able to drop me off that day on the way to the lab, so it wasn't until I walked onto campus that I realized I was in trouble.

At first, I thought I was being called out again for being blond and white. People were hostile in ways that felt familiar after my year at Pasadena High. But I quickly noticed I was being challenged by students of every skin color about my "colors," not my color. Unbeknownst to me, I had inadvertently committed the cardinal sin on John Muir's campus. I had accidentally dressed that morning in the colors of Pasadena High School on Spirit Friday. Muir has school spirit. A whole lot of school spirit. So, what I discovered on that first Friday with this new diverse student body was that even more important than the color of my skin was the fact that I was a clueless red-and-white dissenter from my former high school across town. I walked on campus that day unwittingly advertising for Muir's arch-rival.

Thankfully, when I finally made it to my first-period classroom, weaving through people giving me the stink eye, calling me names, and telling me to go back where I came from, a compassionate classmate who at first had called me out like the rest, ended up lending me her navy blue sweater. I quickly stuffed my red one in my backpack as another student offered to sell me a gold and blue button, declaring, "We are John Muir!" I put it on, surrendering wholeheartedly in that moment to a new perspective, "We are John Muir!" Even with the ongoing, racially motivated encounters I continued to experience over the next three years, I came to recognize there was and still is something special about being a part of the people who call themselves John Muir. It's a rallying cry of identity many of us haven't outgrown. We are kindred spirits.

I feel more connected to Muir than I do my college alma mater. But, besides this second high school experience holding these life-shifting memories for me personally, Muir also appears to be some sort of vortex, as though the universe keeps trying to squeeze out a cosmic message through its halls into the rest of the world.

For instance, many of us graduated with the simple expectation that we would continue to be a part of efforts that moved our world forward. We have many alumni who seem to prove that point by the ways they have distinguished themselves. There's a Hall of Fame on campus at Muir that highlights the different achievements and contributions by alumni in fields such as film, politics, music, sports, literature and science. Current students take heart in the fact that our high school is a jumping-off place for people who have had and will have influence for good in the world.

Probably our most famous alumni are Mack and Jackie Robinson. These two athletic brothers broke barriers and lived in ways that left legacies for future generations. Mathew "Mack" ran in the 1936 Olympics in Berlin, winning the silver medal for the 220-meter race. With other African American athletes that day, Mack helped to destroy Hitler's attempted display of the superiority of whiteness and the Aryan race. Jackie, Mack's younger brother, was hired by the Brooklyn Dodgers in

1947 and broke the color barrier that had kept black athletes from competing in Major League Baseball. My three sons grew up with an art installation of these two brothers in front of Pasadena's iconic city hall.

My classmate Renee Tajima-Peña is an award-winning documentary filmmaker. Her movies are sharp, insightful and persuasive, advocating for change and action. Her film, *No Más Bebés,* shows the stories of immigrant women during the 1960s and 1970s who were sterilized against their will when they were giving birth at the Los Angeles County-USC Medical Center. Renee's list of films draws attention to a variety of American perspectives and civil rights concerns. The focus of her filmmaking and leadership as a professor at UCLA are consistent with the friend I knew at Muir years ago when she was our student body president.

Others from Muir have worked in their own ways to bridge the gaps between people and make the world a better place. A friend since third grade, Colette Cozean, has 100 or more patents for inventions and products that have helped people in America and around the world achieve better health. The clinics she's helped establish in East Africa are life-altering for many communities there. While the hand sanitizer she invented has been hindered by lawsuits incited by competitors, it's an extremely important innovation because it's a rapid, broad-spectrum antiseptic that's persistent and continues to kill bacteria hours after use, even when tested on E. coli and MRSA bacteria.

I'm looking forward to another alum's documentary film screening, still future at this writing. Pablo Miralles is producing *Can We All Get Along?* In it he shares the impact that attending Muir during court-ordered integration had on him. He interviews other alumni and looks at the current resegregation that exists now in America's schools. Pablo's film is titled after a quote by Rodney King, also a Muir alumnus, a troubled guy who nevertheless famously pled for people to behave differently during the Los Angeles Riots. Pablo's documentary is being crowdfunded by many alumni because that phrase communicates so much about the essence of what was cultivated at Muir, a desire not for agreement or sameness but the ability to get along with each other, enjoy life and be better for the journey taken together.

It was good to reconnect during the reunion with the sense of purpose and legacy that exists at Muir. After our weekend of high school reminiscing, I reluctantly left friends and family to move to Louisiana to join Graeme, to work on flood recovery. In spite of the positive attitudes that seemed more prevalent in Louisiana than after previous disasters, our time there seemed more challenging. I felt out of sorts and realized it had to do with revisiting high school memories and our struggles and joys of squarely addressing integration. As students we had genuinely and, as it turned out, prophetically been trying to address the question, "Can we all get along?" I found myself struggling with a sense of being out of place in the South, constantly conscious of our history of slavery and the many nuances of racism.

On a trip back home to Pasadena for a visit in 2017, while still living in Louisiana, I visited the Huntington Library where the works of Octavia Butler were on exhibit. Reminded that Octavia had also been an alumna of John

Muir (1965), I determined to read some of her work. I forgot until I was back in Louisiana when I walked by an end cap in a bookstore displaying Octavia's name big and bold on a shelf dedicated to her book, *Kindred*. Feeling as though the universe was helping me accomplish my good intentions, I bought a copy and was immediately plunged into her story about a black woman and author living in 1976 Pasadena with her white husband.

Octavia's protagonist unexpectedly time travels to the slave-holding South of the early 1800s. Reading about this fictional heroine felt real and familiar, connected to my present geography and my heightened awareness of the plights of slaves who had lived in the same hot, humid, rural Louisiana I was experiencing. I also thought that Octavia's central character seemed like someone I could have known at Muir. Reading my fellow alumna's book while living in Louisiana was emotional in ways I hadn't anticipated.

Kindred is a gripping blend of historical and science fiction storytelling that vividly reveals the tragedy and trauma that came with the nonsensical choice of whites treating other human beings as though they were less than human. I felt caught up in similar present-day contradictions while taking my walks and going about daily life on the ground tilled by slaves, soaked with their tears and blood. The storyline connected my temporary work home in Louisiana with my childhood home in Pasadena.

We can each of us press in to discover ways to identify and psychologically connect to those who are different from us. I have never lived a slave's story, but I have entered into stories like these with my imagination and a desire to understand. I think even the effort to identify with another's experience builds a greater capacity for real-life compassion.

Like the sensations I had as I read Octavia's story in geography that connected me with the essence of the history and emotions that were driving the action of her book, we can seek out those experiences that take us beyond half-hearted, shallow or cursory speculation to places that actually touch our souls and give us a sense of visceral awareness. Anything else might be disingenuous given the importance of these historical components of our history as Americans.

What if we took field trips with our families and friends to places that clearly tell stories different from our own, like Whitney Plantation in Louisiana, Central High School in Little Rock, the Civil Rights Museum at the Lorraine Motel in Memphis, the Chickasaw Cultural Center in Oklahoma, the Manzanar National Historic Site in California and the Tenement Museum in New York? Think of it as a simple way to grow in compassion and understanding of the diversity of our nation. Along the way, include other adventures, experiences and interesting food that will help you remain open and ready to be inspired.

We are at a pivotal time in our history and we can do this present moment differently than previous generations. There is something almost magical about inhabiting the space where a story took place. As you pursue that, you'll learn in ways that history books can't teach. It's important that we imagine ourselves in the skin of another and discover the sensation of being kindred spirits.

One Final Mission

In May 2017, 94-year-old World War II veteran John Seelie raised his right hand and held it to his forehead in a poignant salute to the flag that had flown at Ground Zero in the days following September 11, 2001. Leaning on his friend Diane Pirzada for support, they stood at the 911 Memorial, attended by an honor guard made up of members of the New York Police Department, the Port Authority of New York and New Jersey Police, the Coast Guard and other first responders. John was there to place a lei from Hawaii at the monument in recognition of those who died, those who served and those who survived the day the planes flew into the World Trade Center in New York City.

Like many in the nation, John had been watching the morning news on September 11th at his home in Florida when he saw the report of the attack on New York, the Pentagon and ultimately, the crash in Pennsylvania. Shocked into immobilizing grief by the sight of the twin towers falling, he relived buried emotions from December 7, 1941, when he was serving with the 25th Infantry, stationed at Schofield Barracks near Pearl Harbor. John was 19 that quiet Sunday as enemy planes began bombing and strafing the world around him. With others in his unit, he did all he could with the weapons at hand to stop the two waves of 50 enemy planes that killed many of his friends and destroyed all but two of the 188 planes sitting on the field.

Sixty years later, the old Corporal sat frozen in disbelief, watching on his television screen as another surprise attack of planes wreaked horrendous destruction on his nation. Later, John related to Diane how he hardly left his chair over the next three days, in shock, unable to eat or sleep. Reliving the grief of all he, his friends and the nation had lost when he was young, he wanted to somehow contribute something meaningful at this new time of crisis from his WWII experiences.

In 1941, after the attack on Pearl Harbor, he had gone on to fight on Guadalcanal and New Georgia Island. In 2001, sixty years later, unwilling to sit idly by, John decided on a course of action. He wanted to find a way to encourage the survivors in New York City. As the nation experienced grief, fear and outrage, John worked to design a pin, choosing the picture of the three firefighters raising the American flag on top of the debris the day the towers fell and superimposed the words, "God Bless America. Out of this twisted steel and smoldering ashes America rises." He resolved to go to New York to honor that flag and what it represented about our collective spirit by placing a Hawaiian lei at the site, connecting the two attacks with their shared sense of tragedy and our hopes as a nation.

Inexplicably, the flag went missing almost immediately after it was raised at Ground Zero. While John had some pins made, he didn't make the trip to New York or know how he would fulfill the rest of his original vision.

Years later, the flag was returned and placed in the 911 Memorial. A few months after the flag was restored to the site, John flew to New York with the help of many others who were inspired by his desire to honor the fallen and encourage the survivors. Accompanied by Diane, his friend Mike Cahill, and Emi Kopke, a young artist who was documenting his life in art, John ultimately accomplished his final mission.

During the memorial observance of Fleet Week 2017, just three months before he died, Corporal John Seelie not only offered his respect and thanks but was repeatedly honored for his service in World War II. While he was there, John was finally able to give away hundreds of the pins he designed to veterans, responders, survivors and other Americans he met at the 911 Memorial, at an event on the Intrepid Sea, War and Space Museum, at an event in Grand Central Station and everywhere he went in New York.

Over the years, many have said that rebuilding the World Trade Center at the site of the devastation is a symbol of how America rises again from the loss of lives, peace and property. But near the end of their week in New York, while John, Mike and Diane were on the Staten Island Ferry, they had a significant experience that led them to believe another symbol is both more meaningful and more fitting.

They were standing at the rail together, as John shared his thoughts about the importance of America choosing to live by her ideals. John reminisced about his and other survivors' resilience and the fortitude it required to make it through war. He spoke of the challenges of coming home from the battlefield only to live a life that never feels quite normal again. John's often repeated message was, "Don't be so quick to start another war."

As they stood looking toward Manhattan and the newly constructed tower, John shared his perspective on a bigger picture of war, of what he couldn't see as a young man, how it had been his hatred for the Japanese pilots who had killed his friends at Pearl Harbor that had motivated him as he fought under horrific conditions in the Pacific. He mused about the insanity of war and the painful reality he still carried with him, having poured out his youth, health and dreams on battlefields.

As they talked, Diane drew Mike's and John's attention to a subtle, muted scene out over the water that illustrated what John was sharing. As fog settled in the harbor, Lady Liberty seemed to rise, torch lifted. The freedom she represents became a profound part of this closing chapter of John's story.

Diane described to me how, as they headed back to the dock, John's voice was filled with relief at having accomplished everything he had intended to do in New York. In a tone of quiet peace, he recounted his story again of the time he and others returned to Guadalcanal 50 years after the war. On that trip, he had met and talked with Japanese soldiers who had been on the same battlefields as he had, fighting on the opposite side. John told Diane that what he recognized when he was back in the war zone where so many of his generation had died was how similar their experiences had been as American and Japanese soldiers. Ironically, their differences disappeared. They were old men, looking back together on what they had all suffered when they were young. As they neared the end of their lives, they were able to see what they couldn't in their youth, that ultimately their shared humanity was a stronger connection than the war that had divided them.

Come to the Playground

As a kid, growing up in the quiet foothills of Los Angeles, I loved looking up at the night sky from our backyard and seeing all the points of starlight. Dad would point out the Big Dipper and how to find Polaris, the North Star, off the dipper's rim, and we'd talk about NASA's robotic missions to the planets and what they might discover out there.

When I was about 8, our family went camping one weekend in Joshua Tree, a beautiful part of the California desert. As we put out the fire our first night to go in the tent and crawl into our sleeping bags, I remember looking up from the darkness at the huge dome of sky, stretching from horizon to horizon, brightly saturated with countless, brilliant stars. The physical world suddenly seemed immense and massive. New dimensions were visible. It felt as though millions of planets and swirling galaxies had just come into existence.

Slowly warming up in my sleeping bag, I began questioning my eyes, my senses and the reality they offered me. I had thought I knew the sky, but from the dark geography of the desert, everything was novel. Even my Big

Dipper was hard to recognize. Seeing the limitless points of light showed me that what I had come to know at home had actually been hiding the whole truth. Vast, unexplored mysteries were moving around us all the time.

That equation is still true. There is more we don't know and can't see than what we can. Yet it only takes a quick perusal of any form of media to recognize that many of us don't believe this math and are overly confident in our particular points of view, convinced that what we've learned in our backyards or from our school and work silos affords us enough revelation on reality to declare life's truths in simplistic formulas.

I question folks who think they can single-handedly chart the best course of action for a nation or community like some fictional starship captain who knows all the answers. No one can see that well. Wisdom's path is usually a collaborative discovery made when we come together, recognizing all we don't know, looking at the magnitude and interconnectedness of the mysteries and of what needs solving. It's then that our opinions, skills and abilities can form a powerful, working whole.

Recently I went to a farmer's market in Nashville with my daughter-in-law, Kelly. At a stall where a family was selling creole food-makings, she pointed out a smoked jam she liked, and the two of us ended up in a conversation with them about their food, the joy of sharing family recipes, and hurricanes. They had left New Orleans a day ahead of Katrina, moving north to safety to wait it out. But that hurricane was different than the others they had fled. As they watched the news they discovered they had lost the home, neighborhood and community their family had known for generations. It was a dark time. They moved on to Dallas but eventually decided to rebuild their lives in Nashville and start this business. Disasters and other tragedies sometimes force us out of our expected patterns, sending us in search of a new way through the ruins. Lynn, the self-proclaimed Creole Diva, used destruction as the catalyst for creating a new beginning with her family. They had the same resilient, grateful attitude so many we know in Louisiana have and chose to dream a new dream.

When our three boys were young teenagers, our family worked one summer for a nonprofit in Pennsylvania that helps global workers heal from trauma. Before heading back home after spending a week of vacation doing construction in the sweltering August heat, our family drove to Washington, DC for a few days' enjoyment. There's a picture of our feet encircling the "hallowed spot" on the Lincoln Memorial where Martin Luther King Jr. told the crowd on another hot day in August of the dream he had for America, born from the dark history of segregation and discrimination.

I talked to my guys as we stood there about the importance of living our lives looking for the stories that are bigger than our individual desires and committing ourselves to those things that matter. I didn't want to load them with something heavy as they set out in the years ahead to find themselves and live their own stories. I wanted to inspire them and agree together that our stories would be found in the larger one of freedom and fellowship expressed by King in 1963.

Many consider his speech one of the most moving and encouraging of the twentieth century. Given that President Kennedy would be shot a few months later and we would experience another dark challenge to our hope as a nation, there was an especially prophetic phrase that stood out to me recently. Regarding freedom, equality and justice he said, "Nineteen sixty-three is not an end but a beginning."

As a nation, we have many such beginnings and lessons learned in our hard times. They point us ahead toward the higher ideals we have yet to realize. The best future for America and the world doesn't lie in our past. Our future is not a sequel or a repeat of some former glory. We are in need of crafting something new together, of creating a fresh and relevant vision for the path ahead.

I see a path for Americans that could actually be fun. We could all simply choose to spend time together. It's our best first step toward resilience and the innovative thinking we need. I think we need to take more breaks, not to check texts or social media or binge watch our favorite series but to invest in the same things that motivated us in school—lunch, recess and holidays. I think it's possible to find the playgrounds, both figurative and literal, that already exist in our country and inhabit them more intentionally and more often together. Climbing out of our trenches like the WWI soldiers on Christmas day, we can lay down our weapons. We can leave our old and familiar arguments to hang out together, celebrate and share those things we have in common. I believe we can turn our battlegrounds into playgrounds.

We need to recognize that our individual survival and America's resilience is only possible together. It is possible to find ways to befriend each other and seek ways to end our civil wars.

I've learned something profound as I've stood relaxing and enjoying the huge tanks at the Monterey Aquarium, watching the living displays of the Pacific's delicately balanced ecosystems. The silvery schools of fish, flashing first in one direction and then the next, move as one being, intuitively committed to sticking together to ward off danger. For all their synchrony, the lack of military precision is fascinating. They move in artistic, sweeping entirety, unified, self organizing without a general or other authority among them. Other creatures do the same. Absent any leader, bees make individual and independent decisions that actually lead to the wellbeing of the whole.

Can we as a nation relax our differences to make more space for our stories to be shared and our empathy nurtured? These face-to-face encounters can occur where life happens naturally: restaurants, front porches, public squares, breakrooms and water coolers, movie theaters, farmers' markets, concerts, art exhibits and parks. With playful time together intent on simply being with one another, we're likely to find those joyful rhythms that help us move in ways that result in our wellbeing. We need people in every industry recognizing that the effort they make toward building these kinds of human connections increases our strength and resilience as a nation.

Like that first experience I had looking at the sky away from the city lights, I want us to live humbled by what we don't know, aware that we need to be seekers looking for the treasures that are surely there but still undiscovered.

I'm inviting you to come to the playground. Resilience is relational. Ultimately, no one has it all together, but together we truly have it all.

Acknowledgements

I want to express a lifetime of gratitude to family and friends who made this book possible. Whether I've shared your stories or not, your encouragement, prayers and laughter are much appreciated. Your lives have enriched mine with your presence. Let's keep helping each other stay awake to the importance of caring and friendship.

Thank you, Mom and Dad, for the simple, loving way you've lived. I grew up truly believing that being kind and loving is how normal people do life.

Thank you, Graeme, for 40 years of friendship. I treasure all the ups and downs we've shared. There wouldn't be a disaster business or a book on resilience without you. I'm grateful beyond words that we're doing this adventure together.

Thank you, Andrew, Ryan and Braden. You show good-humored stamina and endurance as I keep figuring out this mom thing. It's a privilege and a lot of fun to be your mum. I'm grateful, Kelly and Kyle, to have two precious daughters now as well.

Thank you, Linda, Karen and Karla, my superhero sisters. I've learned so much from you and your determined journeys seeking to love and do life with full hearts.

Thank you, Amy, your skill as a writing coach gave me courage to share not just stories about disasters, but the relevance of what I've been learning since childhood.

This book, quite literally, wouldn't be *this* book without you.

And thank you, Diane Lynn, connector of people, for finding Amy.

Thank you to our many colleagues in disaster. There's no way to name you all, but we're grateful for everyone.

Thank you, Terrie and Brian, for the multiple ways you've been neighborly over these years as we've come and gone working on disaster, not the least of which were your jocular contributions to this book.

Thank you, readers, for your attention to what I've shared in these pages. It's a gift that you've taken the time.

About the Author

Diane Burden Cox grew up in Pasadena, California in a household that embraced multi-cultural experiences and encouraged global thinking. The product of private and public school education that included court-ordered integration, Diane had opportunity to develop diverse friendships and discover some of the contradictions in American culture.

Diane graduated from University of California, Davis, with graduate studies at California State University, Sacramento, developed curriculum for the Mental Health Association of Los Angeles County, lobbied state representatives for better mental health practices in the state and designed a Mental Health Youth program for the Mental Health Association of California. Diane was a coach, cook, housekeeper, human development expert and K-12 homeschool educator for sons, Andrew, Ryan and Braden.

Diane is CEO of Disaster Scope, Inc., an emergency management consulting firm based in Southern California. She and her husband, Graeme, have lived across the United States, working together on recovery efforts after major disasters.

Index

G

H

I

Iwo Jima, 67

J

Japanese internment camps,
311
Jesus, 29, 50, 68, 91, 92, 129,
188
Jewish, 339
JFO. *See* Joint Field Office (JFO)
John Muir High School, 100, 103,
106, 111, 112, 202, 347, 348,
350, 351, 352
Joint Field Office (JFO), 144, 315
Jones
Dr. Lucy, 220
Silvia, 201
Journey to Independence, 181
Joyeux Noel, 7
Jurassic World Exodus, 297

K

Katrina
documentary, 174
stories, 121
Kennedy, John F., 30, 363
Kennedy, Robert, 91
Kent State, 87
Kindness, 81, 85, 87, 98, 125,
200, 210, 270
Kindred, 352
King, Dr. Martin Luther, Jr., 15,
50, 67, 188, 363
King, Rodney, 199, 351
Kivengere, Festo, 93, 115, 195
Kopke, Emi, 357
Ku Klux Klan, 70, 333
Kumbaya, 298

L

Lake Avenue Congregational, 56
Langteaux, James, 253

Leader, 7, 69, 172, 176, 261, 365
church, 90
community, 165
India, 270
political, 21, 240
protest, 256
religious, 340
Leadership, 81, 101, 102, 116,
166
Learning disabilities, 183
Leave It To Beaver, 77
Lee, Dr. Dan, 47
Levitt, Joseph Gordon, 133
Liberty, 69, 70, 110, 111
Little Rock
Central High School National
Historic Site Visitor
Center, 100
Nine, 100
Lord of the Flies, 101
Lorraine Motel, 353
Los Angeles
Foodshed, 251
riots, 199, 221
Louisiana Spring Flood, 254
Love, 56, 63, 80, 90, 92, 121,
125, 126, 183, 184, 200, 210,
224, 235, 263, 270, 298
country, 94, 287
family, 284, 286
forgiveness, 95
God, 91, 186
neighborly, 314
of learning, 221
perfect, 116
radical, 60
revolutionary, 93
song, 53
summer of, 87
types, 210
voice of, 188
Love Does, 281
Luwum, Janani, 93

M

N

O

P